Shortcuts for Accenting Your Garden

Over 500 Easy and Inexpensive Tips

A Garden Way Publishing Book

STOREY

Storey Communications, Inc.

Schoolhouse Road

Pownal, Vermont 05261

*The mission of Storey Communications is to serve our customers
by publishing practical information that encourages personal independence
in harmony with the environment.*

Cover design by Cindy McFarland
Cover photograph by Jerry Pavia
Text design by Michelle Arabia
Text production by Carol J. Jessop
Edited by Sandra Webb
Line drawings by Judy Eliason, except on page 58 by Ann M. Poole
Indexed by Nan N. Badgett, Word•a•bil•ity

Printed in the United States by Capital City Press
10   9   8   7   6   5   4   3

Garden Way Publishing was founded in 1973 as part of the Garden Way Incorporated Group of Companies, dedicated to bringing gardening information and equipment to as many people as possible. Today the name "Garden Way Publishing" is licensed to Storey Communications, Inc., in Pownal, Vermont. For a complete list of Garden Way Publishing titles call 1-800-827-8673. Garden Way Incorporated manufactures products in Troy, New York, under the Troy-Bilt® brand including garden tillers, chipper/shredders, mulching mowers, sicklebar mowers, and tractors. For information on any Garden Way Incorporated product, please call 1-800-345-4454.

Library of Congress Cataloging-in-Publication Data

Binetti, Marianne, 1956–
    Shortcuts for accenting your garden : over 500 easy and inexpensive tips / Marianne Binetti.
        p.   cm.
    "A Garden Way Publishing book."
    Includes bibliographical references and index.
    ISBN 0-88266-830-7 (hc) — ISBN 0-88266-829-3 (pb)
    1. Landscape gardening.   I. Title.
SB473.B5   1993
712'.6—dc20
                                 92-54654
                                     CIP

To my favorite garden accents, Angela, Tony, and Alisa,
who really know how to liven up a landscape;
and with thanks to Joe for helping to write this book.

CHAPTER 1

Organization: Make the Most of What You Have

SHORTCUT:

*Get organized —
or at least give others
the illusion that
there's a method
to your planting
madness.*

Envision the joy and beauty of a lovely garden. No wonder God plunked Adam and Eve down in Eden! Everyone wants a lovely landscape, but finding the time to create a personal Eden is difficult. For most would-be paradise planners, the hardest step to take is the first one. The decision about where to start, what plants to buy, and where to position pathways can be overwhelming. But there is a shortcut to all this indecision: it's called organization.

Putting Your Dreams on Paper

Organizing your outdoor space doesn't mean you have to attack the property with tape measure and graph paper (although if this weren't a book about shortcuts, that wouldn't be a bad idea). Trade in the measuring tape for a library card and check out the garden and landscape section. If you want an even quicker route to landscape ideas, scoop up some shelter magazines at the nearest drugstore. (Shelter mags are the home and decorating publications filled with glossy photos of perfect home interiors. They also include creative treatments of house exteriors and landscaping.)

Collecting ideas about the plants that do well in your climate is as easy as taking a drive through a neighborhood of fine homes. Better yet, park the car, grab a notebook, and take a stroll through that neighborhood with the impressive-looking front yards. Write down any idea that grabs your attention. This is no time to be practical about what you can afford or what fits with the style of your house. Recording ideas about what appeals to you and what grows well in your area is a pleasant way to begin the organization process. There's so much to choose from, and deciding what you like is an easy way to eliminate a lot of the choices, and thus, a lot of the confusion. What you're after is a landscape style or look that will give some direction to your future gardening plans. This is also a good time to visit a show garden or lavish public garden. The more landscape styles you observe, the closer you'll come to discovering the style of landscape design that appeals to you the most. It doesn't really matter that the formal rose garden you love in the park takes up half an acre and your entire yard covers a fraction of that space: Your master plan can include instead a *tiny* formal rose garden laid in a sunny spot in your yard.

Let's take time for a reality check here and come clean with the fact that organization and planning do take time. A master plan is great, but what you really need is an instant shortcut to fill up the empty space around your new house or the void left around your older home after you've ripped out overgrown shrubs. Many homeowners simply want to get something in the ground right away before the weeds take over. And, as long as we're being practical, let's also assume that this temporary quick fix has to be as inexpensive as possible. Now, listen to this story about how a simple idea helped supplement a very modest landscaping budget and gave quick cover to an empty yard.

A young couple had moved into their first home, which had a tiny front yard and no landscaping. They had spent all their savings to buy the house, so adding trees and shrubs for the landscape had to wait. The female half of this couple was one of my many sisters, so I can attest that the couple were definitely greenhorns in the green thumb department. It would take them a while to organize and to decide just what kind of landscape and plants they liked. Meanwhile, the weeds were coming up fast, so a tiny bit of sod was laid down to serve as a front lawn, which about blew the money allotted for landscaping. But, there were beds to fill around the lilliputian lawn, and this is where a lack of funds worked to an attractive advantage. Frugality often fathers beautifully simple designs.

The month was June, and a local greenhouse was having a closeout sale on bedding plants. Armed with a $10 bill and a budding desire to have a front yard in flower, the couple purchased 10 six-packs of hot-pink petunias. They came home with change in their pockets and 60 tiny petunias that needed planting.

Their new trilevel home had a tiny balcony in the front of the house with a sill just wide enough for a narrow window box. The small slab of cement that made up the front porch had just enough room to hold a few clay pots. The wooden planter box and the clay pots were mismatched hand-me-downs, so before filling these humble containers with penny-pinching petunia plants, both were painted with the Cape Cod gray paint the builder had left after doing the house.

You can probably imagine the colorful end to this temporary landscaping solution. The pink petunias

QUICK TIP FOR MORE COLOR

To load your petunias with blossoms, pinch back half of the new growth once the young plants are 6 inches tall. Fertilize with a water-soluble plant food, according to label instructions. (Mark future fertilizing dates on your calendar so you won't forget.) Give the petunias a spot where they'll get at least half a day of sunshine. Stand back for the explosion of color that will follow in a few weeks. Snip off 6-inch lengths of petunias every few weeks to use as cut flowers. This will keep the plants bushy and blooming until frost.

stood out handsomely against the gray house, dripping from the boxes on the balcony and filling the collection of freshly painted pots on the porch. More petunias edged the tiny patch of lawn, and the pink border made the grass appear even greener than it was. Perfect strangers stopped to compliment the young couple on their lovely landscape. By midsummer, it was obvious that the bargain pink petunias had grown into a beautiful shortcut to a showcase garden.

Bedding plants may be the easiest way for beginning gardeners to temporarily fill the empty space of a new landscape, but experienced gardeners know that growing plants from seed is still the best bargain for your buck. You don't even need to buy the seed if you're outgoing enough to meet your garden-loving neighbors.

Let me introduce you to another sister who also moved into a new home devoid of any landscaping except a sad-looking weeping willow stuck in the backyard. Plans for a lovely landscape were started immediately, but purchase of the flowering trees and blooming shrubs would have to wait. But, that didn't

OTHER EASY-TO-GROW AND EASY-TO-FIND ANNUAL BEDDING PLANTS

For Sun
Geranium
Marigold
Nasturtium
Zinnia

For Shade
Coleus
Fibrous begonia
Impatiens
Lobelia

mean the yard would sit empty. Two weeks after moving into the neighborhood, my sister paid a visit to the grandmotherly woman with a flower-filled garden who lived across the street. Like most gardeners, this neighbor was generous and quickly offered cuttings and divisions of her many perennials, as well as a jar full of home-harvested flower seeds.

Perennial flowers are wonderful because they return year after year, but because perennials often live so long, a new homeowner is forced to make quick decisions about their planting location — and often regrets the decision later on when a more mature landscape begins to take shape. Most perennials also need good soil preparation — a time-consuming process that involves loosening of the soil and adding of compost or of manure. A much more practical choice as a gift for the new landscape was the jar of tiny seeds that my sister's neighbor sent home with her after the get-acquainted visit. In a few months, the collection of home-harvested flower seeds turned the once-bare landscape into a yard full of color. The wise neighbor had supplied my sister with thousands of candytuft and cosmos seeds. The candytuft was the easy-to-grow annual variety *(Iberis umbellata)* that bloomed only a few months after planting. The candytuft seeds sprouted with enthusiasm wherever they were tossed and bloomed in shades of pink, lavender, and purple. The cosmos seeds *(Cosmos bipinnatus)* matured more slowly, so the tall, feathery plants were filling in and blooming around the new landscape by midsummer just as the candytuft blossoms were beginning to fade.

After a year or two, this temporary landscape of cosmos and candytuft began to change as a master plan was developed and shrubs and trees were purchased. A rose garden eventually replaced the wildflower look that the self-seeding annual flowers had given the yard. The blooming landscape may have been temporary, but I imagine the smug smile on the generous neighbor's face was permanent. Instead of staring at a new house surrounded by dirt and weeds, she had flowers to look at — the blooming offspring of her own plants!

The moral of these two stories is neither to corner the market on pink petunias and wait for compliments from passing strangers, nor to beg your neighbors for surplus seeds and put in a quick and inexpensive flower garden. Landscaping with bedding plants and flower seeds is a colorful but temporary solution to the lack of funds that plagues many new homeowners. The point of these examples is that using annual flowers to fill an empty space is a shortcut to buy you time while

Candytuft and cosmos are two annuals that are easy to grow from seed.

you work on developing a more substantial landscape plan and learn about the style of garden that appeals to you the most.

The first example about the pink petunias is also meant to show how effective a simple design can be. Choosing one plant of one color helped to organize the tiny front yard and give it a showy, tidy look. This brings us back to the shortcut stated at the beginning of this chapter: Get organized.

You don't need to lock yourself into a single planting style or have a collection of monotone plants to appear organized. Even avid plant collectors who buy specimen plants because they like the way they look at the nursery can organize and improve their landscapes. Let me illustrate how a few minor moves and transplants can work to organize a hodgepodge collection of shrubs in a mature landscape.

This garden story is about Zoe, an enthusiastic and experienced plant collector who lives across the river from us on a beautiful 5-acre spread. This woman has a passion for dwarf evergreen shrubs and unique specimen trees. She also likes to buy rhododendrons by the dozen and to order perennial plants if the name or color catches her fancy. The main complaint that Zoe had about her landscape was that it confused her every time she looked out the window. "There's no rhyme or reason to this mess," is how she stated the problem. She

FILLING IN THE SPACE WITH FLOWERS
GROWN FROM SEED

❖ You can't just sprinkle seeds about your yard and wait for flowers to pop up. Growing plants from seed takes some soil preparation, even if the seeds you plant are of the wildflower type that don't require fertile soil. The seeds germinate easier if you loosen or hoe the soil, remove rocks and pieces of debris, and check daily to make sure the soil stays moist while the seedlings are sprouting.

❖ One advantage of sprinkling seeds around a new yard is that you can soon tell where your soil is good and where it needs improvement just by comparing the size of the plants that come up. Start with a package of wildflower seeds if you don't have any experienced gardeners in the neighborhood to offer you the local self-sowing favorites.

❖ The flowers that are easiest to grow from seed include marigold, lobelia, alyssum, nasturtium, sweet pea, cosmos, annual candytuft, bachelor's button, pot marigold, and pansy.

❖ Either wait until the danger of frost has passed to sow the seeds directly into the ground or start them earlier indoors on the windowsill and transplant outdoors when the plants are a few inches tall.

❖ During the first week or two, cover newly transplanted seedlings with newspaper tents or another type of protection from nighttime cold and daytime heat until they harden off.

❖ Thin out the seedlings to at least 6 inches apart. You may be able to transplant the extras to another part of the yard. A baby's spoon is a good tool to use for such delicate digging and planting work.

asked me to offer landscaping advice and to suggest placement of the dozens of plants still in pots that needed planting.

Zoe had plants that sat in pots for over a year while she thought about where to dig the planting hole. Fortunately for the potted specimens, she was a dependable care giver and rarely lost a potted plant-in-waiting.

In such a case, a design plan for a plant collector is not as simple as surrounding the lawn with a row of shrubs. Zoe and I worked out a series of paths that connected groups of trees and shrubs. The largest trees on the property became the focal points for each collection or minigarden. By labeling these groups of shrubs with titles such as Japanese Garden, Juniper Collection, Fall Foliage Garden, and Dwarf Evergreen Area, we gave the property the look of an arboretum or public park. Often, the rearrangement of plants already in a garden is a shortcut to better organization.

The mixed collection of unusual plants, now organized into groups, became more pleasant to view, simplified the maintenance, and, most important, made it easier for Zoe to decide where to plant her new acquisitions.

IDEAS FOR ORGANIZING A YARD OF SHRUBS

❖ The biggest or most difficult-to-move shrub should become the focal point of the collection. For example, if you have a tall, narrow juniper in the middle of the lawn that looks out of place, clear the lawn away from this specimen plant and add a collection of low-growing shrubs to create an island of evergreen color.

❖ Organize a collection using the color of the foliage for inspiration instead of the type of plant. Rather than planting different varieties of junipers around one tall specimen, collect evergreens with blue needles or red foliage to match the unusual foliage color of your focal plant. A good example of this is a purple-leaved smoke tree *(Cotinus coggygria)* used as the centerpiece in an island of burgundy-leaved barberry *(Berberis thunbergii* 'Atropurpurea') and a gracefully weeping red Japanese maple *(Acer palmatum* 'Ornatum'). Large gray boulders used throughout the planting are a nice contrast.

❖ A seasonal display is another way to group together otherwise unrelated plant specimens. Early-blooming shrubs such as quince, forsythia, and witch hazel can become the winter-blooming garden collection, and suddenly, it is easy to decide where the early-blooming crocus and snowdrop bulbs should be planted.

❖ Plant form can also inspire plant collections. Imagine the skinny, upright look of a skyrocket juniper surrounded by smaller shrubs that echo its pointed shape. 'Pyramidalis' arborvitae and dwarf Alberta spruce are two shrubs that would make the point handsomely. Weeping forms such as those found on grafted lace-leaved maples or dwarf weeping birch can also be used as the focus of a collection. Plant collectors who are running out of room might want to focus on dwarf shrubs and miniature plants.

The last time I ran into Zoe was at a nursery, and she was up to her old tricks again, buying exquisite dwarf evergreens while admitting that she still had potted purchases at home that she hadn't gotten around to planting. But, at least now she had some idea about where to place them — when she got around to it.

Determining Your Garden Style

Plants aren't the only part of a landscape that adds to the showcase look once they've been organized. The choice of a garden style can dress up the exterior of your home in much the same way that a theme or furniture style describes a well-designed interior. Look around at your indoor furnishings. Most homeowners lean toward a certain furniture style that can be described as country or traditional, as opposed to contemporary or Oriental. Of course, a mixture of many furniture and interior styles (labeled "eclectic" by interior designers) is also attractive, but the most beautiful and comfortable spaces have a dominant decorating theme that organizes the look of the room. The same design idea can be used with your exterior. By choosing a garden style or theme, you narrow down your choices and take a shortcut to a more organized landscape.

The plants you choose, the paving material, the fence style, and most important, the style of your home's exterior, all give your garden a certain style. Decide what type of landscape you would like and then keep that style in mind whenever you have the chance to make improvements or choose materials for your landscape. Let me describe five of the most common landscape styles that are used repeatedly in showcase gardens of the world. I refer to these styles throughout the book and offer shortcuts to achieving each style with specific focal points, fences, paths, and plants.

THE FORMAL/ESTATE STYLE

This is the yard with the pristine lawn and right angles of rectangular flowerbeds accented with perfectly clipped evergreens. The flowers are neat and uniform in shape and color. Roses, geraniums, boxwood hedges, and symmetrical trees placed all in a row are favorites for the formal look. Pathways are paved in cement, perhaps with a bit of brick edging, and focal points are formal statues, sundials, fountains, and birdbaths with a lot of detail. Pots are decorative terra-cotta or urn-shaped cement in the Greek Revival style. One example is the formal gardens at the famous Butchart Gardens in British Columbia, Canada, where they call this formal area the Italian Gardens.

The formal, symmetrical style of this landscape looks best around homes with a similar exterior. Colonial, Victorian, or country homes are good candidates for formal front yards. (Of course, if you live on an estate with an iron gate and stone lions guarding the steps to the front door, your house would be well complemented by the formal style, but it would be your gardener who would be reading this book of shortcuts, not you.)

*The formal/estate style is characterized by a pristine lawn,
clipped evergreens, and symmetrical flowerbeds.*

Even small yards around modest homes can be landscaped with the estate look if you're a gardener who prefers straight lines, symmetrical plants, and a perfectly maintained lawn. But, you better have a lot of time and energy on your hands to maintain it. It is no coincidence that the formal style is popular among wealthy estate owners who can afford to hire the garden maintenance out to professionals.

COUNTRY/COTTAGE STYLE

A mixture of blooming shrubs and perennial flowers, stone or brick pathways, and lattice and picket-fence lines characterize the popular country or cottage gardening style. Climbing roses, perennials, petunias, pansies, lilacs, and blooming trees are the favored plants used to create this landscaping mood. Charming focal points such as gazebos, birdhouses, arches, and iron and wood benches highlight the more casual style of the country look. Large homes with wraparound porches, or small bungalows with dormer windows and a cottage look, are both perfectly suited to the country-style garden.

The country/cottage style has a mixture of blooming shrubs and perennial flowers and charming focal points like arches and birdbaths.

CONTEMPORARY/ORIENTAL STYLE

Low-growing evergreen shrubs, specimen plants such as lace-leaved maples and carefully pruned pines, and paths of fine pebbles with dry streambeds and large boulders set among moss reflect a contemporary garden style. Ornamental grasses and other drought-resistant plants are also favored, and the look is restrained, with a lot of space between plants. The clean lines and open feeling are much the same as the ones you get from a living room done in contemporary style. But, instead of bare white walls and a single piece of modern art, the contemporary landscape features a pool of gravel and stones with one pine tree gently leaning nearby. This is the yard that could get by with a patch of woolly thyme or Irish moss ground cover in the front yard instead of the traditional grass lawn. Contemporary/Oriental style landscapes complement houses with flat or angular rooflines or with contemporary wood-and-glass facades.

The contemporary/Oriental style is characterized by a staggered walkway, weeping evergreens, groups of azaleas, and focal points like stone pagodas.

NATURALISTIC/WOODLAND STYLE

Nature lovers who enjoy the mixed jungle feeling of draping greenery and plant-covered ground love woodland or native plant landscapes with a lot of ferns, azaleas, pathways lined with logs and wood chips, and rustic focal points such as cedar birdhouses and animals or wooden poles carved from logs. The borders in a woodland garden are made of split-rail fences or rows of native trees and shrubs. Hollowed-out stumps and old wheelbarrows or other rustic, recycled containers may serve as containers for blooming annuals.

The best homes for this casual style of landscape design are those set among trees, such as a log cabin or a house with a wood-shingle exterior, but any home with stained wood siding blends in with a woodland garden. As for maintenance, this style wins the award for needing the least. Homeowners with little time or inclination for fussing with flowers should consider going back to nature with native plants.

The naturalistic/woodland style uses native plants, ferns, and rustic focal points like hollowed-out stumps filled with blooming annuals.

MEDITERRANEAN/DESERT STYLE

Owners of adobe or stucco houses in the sun belt can avoid much landscape maintenance by planning their yards around a desert or sunshine theme. Drought-resistant plants native to the area, such as cacti, ornamental grasses, succulents, and a few trees, blend well with the boulders, stones, and gravel that cover most of the surface in this type of garden. Colorful pottery and fences of wooden poles or adobe walls look great with this landscape style. Tile surfaces are used for paths and courtyards, and focal points can be as casual as a wooden wagon wheel or as elaborate as a tiled, tiered water fountain.

Low-roofed ramblers or homes with a western U.S. look are also complemented by the Mediterranean garden style. You don't even need to live in an arid area to plan this type of garden. Water-wise landscapes are attractive even in my home state of Washington, where we want outsiders to think it rains and drizzles most of the year.

Don't worry if your image of a showplace garden doesn't fit neatly into any of these five major styles. The arbitrarily chosen styles outlined here are loose definitions of the many diverse garden styles that make U.S. landscapes so rich and varied.

Think of these garden styles as tools for planning your dream garden. By labeling your ideas with a descriptive name, you can narrow down your choices of wonderful plants and features. The labeling of a garden style isn't meant to limit your ideas or choice of plants. It should serve instead as a source of inspiration and organization to point you in the direction of compatible plants and materials. Getting organized by choosing a garden style is the first step in planning your showcase garden.

The Mediterranean/desert style has boulders, gravel walkways,
cacti, ornamental grasses, and terra-cotta pots of flowers.

My own garden is a good example of a minicollection of the five basic styles. My family and I live on 2 acres of mostly wooded land in the Pacific Northwest. The mild, moist climate allows for a tremendous variety of plant material, and I have an uncontrollable urge to try to grow it all. The traditional style of our house helps determine which plants go where. The brick pathways and circular brick courtyard in the front were inspired by the brick trim on the front of the house. The pathways and courtyard, in turn, helped determine the small but formal rose garden near the driveway and the formal brass sundial in the middle of the brick courtyard. Formal rows of annuals line the front brick path, but casual-looking hedges of rhododendrons and azaleas hold back the forest from the curves of the front lawn.

The front yard may be formal and traditional to match the front of the house, but the backyard has a rustic woodland garden, the east side has a contemporary area, and the west side a traditional perennial border.

One more landscaping style should be mentioned. It's called Early Backyard Playground. Swing sets, tree houses, and plastic wading pools are the focal points that dramatize the design of this early childhood look. In our landscape, the back patio leads directly to the playground garden. Some very practical features in this part of the yard include raised rocks around the flowerbeds and cement walls around the vegetable garden area to serve as bumpers for wayward soccer balls. The five raised vegetable garden beds (one for each member of the family) are edged with a 4-inch-wide concrete wall — just the right height to sit on while weeding. No garden design should overlook the basic facts that your kids need a place to play and that you may want to use the sunniest spot of the yard for growing vegetables.

Take a look now at your own yard and think about what style of landscape will best show off your home. Let the style help to guide and to organize your planting and outside decorating. Always feel free to add ideas from other landscaping styles and, above all, use your backyard or private areas to make your home more comfortable for outdoor living. Following are some suggestions to guide you:

❖ A low-roofed rambler might look best with a contemporary landscape style. A split-rail fence or post-and-board fence across the front echoes the long, horizontal lines of a sprawling one-story house.

❖ A tall, narrow house such as the row houses found in large cities are best displayed by a more traditional landscape design that includes tall, narrow evergreens or skinny trees. An Italian cypress or a yew at the corner or a flowering cherry tree with an upright growth habit are examples of the tree shape that complements a high roofline.

❖ Homes with brick trim can be tied to the landscape by use of similar brick to edge walkways or build planters. Victorian homes can carry off the formal landscape style, which includes urns and latticework arches. Contemporary houses with a lot of angles should echo that feel with beds and pathways that meet at angles.

Right away, you are probably muttering to yourself that your house has no identifiable style. It may be plain and boxy or a multilevel structure with a complex roofline but nothing else to distinguish it. Don't waste energy worrying that your home lacks character. You can add a landscape that will make any habitat ooze with character and shout with style. Notice how the plain little box of a house in the drawings became something totally different depending on what type of landscape style was used to transform it.

Organization is the first step toward a showcase garden, and each of the following chapters teaches you more ways to organize and turn your own yard into a showplace — all by taking shortcuts.

Where to Begin

I'm not going to let the procrastinators among you have any excuse for not getting started with your landscape improvement. It's easy to set your priorities and structure your exterior decorating. Begin your decorating plans at the front entrance, continue around to the back patio or deck, and work your way toward the outer edges of the yard until you add the fence lines and borders, accents, and focal points.

❖ Start with the front entrance. Does the walkway need to be wider? Will painting the front door, adding pots of flowers, or clearing out the overgrown shrubbery improve the first impression? Painting, pruning, and paving should be priorities.

❖ The backyard living area and the size and shape of the deck or patio need to be considered next. A formal landscape style usually calls for a symmetrical deck or patio, whereas a contemporary, angled surface complements the clean line of a more modern house. Continue to prune overgrown shrubbery from the windows and work on pathways.

❖ The trees and shrubs need to be located so that they can be enjoyed from the windows and serve functions such as cooling the house, offering privacy, and adding seasonal color. This is when you get to visit the nursery and add to your plant collection. You already have the patios and pathways finished, so adding plants and working on the lawn come next.

❖ Finishing up fence lines and borders, framing the lawn with an edging strip, and adding decorative accents such as sundials, water features, and birdbaths are the fun parts you save until the end.

SUREFIRE SHORTCUTS

❖ Buy a notebook and write *Garden Ideas* on the front. Visit nurseries and garden centers and jot down the names of plants that you like. Collect pictures from shelter magazines to add to the notebook.

❖ Visit a show garden, drive through an interesting neighborhood, or check out a collection of garden design books from the library. Record the garden styles that appeal to you the most in your garden notebook.

❖ Choose one section of the yard to work on at a time. Break down any job into smaller, more manageable steps so that you are less likely to become overwhelmed and to use confusion as an excuse to do nothing. If you tend to procrastinate, inspire yourself to act by setting a date for outdoor entertaining. List everything you would like to accomplish before your guests arrive. (It's always good for the ego to show off before-and-after photos.)

❖ Determine which part of the yard is the least visible. Use this section to store sickly plants, bags of peat moss, compost piles, and recycled materials that you intend to use in your garden.

❖ Choose a section of the yard with the best soil and an access to water; improve the soil with peat moss. Use this as a holding bin for baby plants and displaced plant material while you figure out where new plants should go.

❖ Don't buy plants and then wander aimlessly about wondering where to put them. Choose a location first, then look for a plant that suits the space, soil, and sun conditions of the available site. Plan your plant parenthood only after a thorough home study and honest evaluation of how much time you can afford to devote to their care and upbringing.

Most-Asked Questions about Organization

Q. *We have moved into our new house and are ready to start landscaping; the problem is that my husband and I are total opposites when it comes to landscape style. I would love a country-style garden with rambling roses, hollyhocks, and other perennial flowers, and I prefer curved or natural-looking pathways with a small lawn in front. However, my husband is a perfectionist, and he insists on straight lines and geometrically pruned shrubs. At our last home, he even measured the spacing of the shrubs so that they would all be exactly the same distance from each other. He spent every weekend fussing over the lawn and pruning his evergreen shrubs, but we had very little color. How can we work out a compromise?*

A. Your problem is not unique. There must be a reason why so many married couples like the exact opposite styles of landscaping. (I often act as referee when I make a yard call to a new landscape.) I consider it fate that opposites attract and suggest that the landscape will benefit if each of you adds elements that you love. Neither of you is right or wrong in your preference of style. A homeowner's landscape should please the owners no matter what their tastes.

Now that I've gracefully navigated around a potential marriage land mine, let's get to work charting a new direction. Let the front yard lean toward the formal look. The pathway to the front door can please your husband with perfect symmetry and evenly spaced shrubs. As you get away from the doorway, however, allow the design to become more casual. Blooming shrubs with a graceful growth habit such as the old-fashioned rambling roses, lilacs, and forsythias that you love can be used at the border of the property. Group them together so that your snip-happy husband will know that this area is off-limits to his pruning shears. A boxwood hedge below some windows or alongside a driveway should satisfy his desire to clip and control.

In the backyard, continue with the plan to keep the more formal look close to the house, growing tidy shrubs such as azaleas and dwarf evergreens near the patio. Enthusiastic vines such as wisteria, clematis, and honeysuckle should be far away from the house on their own arbor. Your flower-filled perennial garden will always look messy and out of control to your husband, so choose a location on the side of the house or some other out-of-sight area that you can call your own. Adding a strong border such as brick or cement curbing around the perennial bed helps give it a more tidy and ordered look. If your backyard is long and deep, try dividing it in half with a hedge of blooming shrubs or a low split-rail fence. Build an arched entryway that connects the formal half of the backyard with the blooming back half of the property. Now, you both can design and maintain the garden of your dreams.

Q. *Our home is painted peach with teal trim, and I would like to use flowers in window boxes and flower pots that complement this color scheme. I have seen roses in apricot and peach, but are there any teal flowers for container gardening?*

A. Color coordinating your house and plants shouldn't limit you to teal and peach blossoms. If you want to organize your summer blooming display with color, keep in mind that many orange and yellow flowers look wonderful blooming side by side as a peach substitute. Consider hot orange geraniums and gold and orange marigolds for planters in the sun, with trailing blue-green lotus vines to give a touch of teal.

Flowers for the shady window box include wax begonias and tuberous begonias in many orange and apricot shades, impatiens, and both upright and trailing fuchsias. Impatiens give you the most bloom for your buck. They flower best in shade, but if given plenty of water, they also bloom all summer in sun. New varieties of impatiens come in apricot as well as in orange. Check the glossy photos of seed catalogs to order the exact color you want if you don't find peach-hued bedding plants at your garden center.

For early spring color, fill your pots and window boxes with apricot pansies, primroses, and orange and salmon tulips. Gold crocuses and dwarf yellow daffodils also have the rich, warm colors you are looking for and bloom very early in spring. Once fall arrives, you have a full range of yellow, gold, and apricot colors to choose from when potted mums go on sale. Use teal paint to trim your window boxes and planters, and don't forget that you can add touches of white for contrast. Sweet alyssum and white lobelia are two low-growing annual flowers that work well to highlight any color scheme you choose.

Chapter Summary

❖ Getting organized is the first shortcut to good design. New homeowners can fill the empty space with fast-growing bedding plants or self-sowing flowers to buy time while planning and saving for their dream garden.

❖ If you pick a garden style that complements your house and your personal style, you'll be taking a shortcut when it comes to deciding on plant and material choices in the future.

❖ Five types of garden styles are suggested:

Formal/estate
Country/cottage
Contemporary/Oriental
Naturalistic/woodland
Mediterranean/desert

CHAPTER 2

Porches, Pots, Paint, and Courtyards: Quick Steps to a Showcase Welcome

> **SHORTCUT:**
>
> *Focus on improving the front walkway and doorway garden area for a maximum return on your home improvement investment.*

Your first steps toward a new or renovated landscape should be giant ones — that are easy to take. Quick shortcuts with paint and pots move you quickly down the path of landscape improvement toward a showcase garden. The other necessary (and very worthwhile) projects, such as renovating a lawn and planting a hedge, just don't give the instant gratification that a few hours' work on the entry area bring. Get yourself pumped up for a total landscape overhaul by starting with something impressive but easy to do — improving your entry.

Decorating the front entrance is like wrapping a present. When you add excitement to the exterior package, what's inside suddenly seems more valuable. Although any landscape improvements to the front or public part of your property show generosity to the neighborhood, it is the entry area that shows appreciation and honor to your own guests. (It is also the quickest way to impress prospective house buyers or bank appraisers.) Dressing up the entrance and walkway to the front door is a surefire shortcut to landscape improvement. Just take one step outside, and you're already on top of this impressionable improvement project.

Let's face it, most people have such impersonal front doors and entry gardens that they might as well serve as the gateway to a business office. We express our personal tastes when decorating our living room or bedroom, so why should our home's exterior entrance look bland?

Creating a front entrance that is welcoming without being overpowering is a challenge no more daunting than furnishing the living area inside your home in your own personal taste. You want comfort, beauty, and a little drama or style to appear in both the indoor living room and the outdoor welcoming room. It doesn't matter if your outdoor welcoming room is nothing but a cement pad and a plain door. Treat it like an empty canvas waiting to be decorated with paint, flowers, and eye-catching accents. These improvements are the first things that guests notice about your landscaping as they enter your home.

You may be partial to subtle colors and modern accents, or you may express yourself with country charm or Victorian flourish. These preferences should be displayed near your front door. You need to consider the style of your house and garden when you make plans to punch up your entry, but no matter what style you're after, every front entrance can be improved by taking advantage of these four shortcuts to a more successful welcome:

❖ Add more color with container gardens or paint.

❖ Widen the pathway or walkway to the front entrance.

❖ Interject your own personality with accents.

❖ Illuminate the scene with added light for safety and drama.

Adding More Color

POTS FOR PORCH DRESSING

Adding color with container gardens near the front door is the quickest way to dress up an entrance. This is undoubtedly why so many homeowners hang their summer bloomers from the front porch or set a pot of geraniums on the stoop. Consider these tips to make the most of your porch pots:

❖ Use a family of matching pots on the porch or near the entryway. A trio of mama-, papa-, and baby-sized pots all in the same color make a harmonious group.

❖ If you have room for only one pot of colorful flowers, put it on a pedestal. Turn a matching pot upside down or use a plant stand to raise your potted plants closer to chest level. Raised planters are easier to care for and to look at.

❖ If you don't have the porch space for even one pot, hang a trio off to the side. By hanging three pots one right under the other (or one hanging from the bottom of the other), you create a pyramid of plants but have to water only the top one. Let the water flow out of its drainage holes and into the plants below.

Moss baskets look spectacular because the plants encompass the container and give it the look of a hanging bouquet of flowers. The moss and the wire frame can be used year after year. There is one important rule to remember: never let the baskets dry out! They need fertilizer and water more often than other types of hanging baskets because they drain so quickly. Moss baskets growing in full sun may need watering twice a day.

Following are some good plants for hanging moss baskets that receive half a day of sun:

Brachycome (Swan River daisy)
Browallia (amethyst flower)
Campanula (bellflower)
Lantana
Lobelia
Petunia (multiflora varieties with small but numerous blossoms)
Sanvitalia (creeping zinnia)
Schizanthus (also known as poor man's orchid)
Torenia (wishbone flower)
Verbena

Petunias and schizanthus are good for use on the top of the basket because they tend to grow up and over the edge. You can also plant a spectacular display using just one type of flower. Space the plants 4 to 6 inches apart around the sides and across the top of the container.

Even if you don't use a moss basket on your porch or a trio of hanging planters stacked one over the other, try to position all your hanging baskets over

HOW TO MAKE A HANGING MOSS BASKET

Hanging moss baskets are the showiest of all container gardens, with flowers spilling from the top and sides of the moss-covered wire frame, hiding the container. The wire frames come in many shapes; some are even flat on one side for hanging against a wall. Here's how you can make your own hanging moss basket:

1. You need sphagnum moss to line the wire basket. This type of moss is sold at greenhouses and craft supply stores, usually in bale form. Moisten the moss by dipping it in a bucket of water before using it. (If you gather your own moss from the floor of a forest, be sure to spread it out on newspaper outdoors and overnight so that most of the insects can escape.)

2. Lay sections of moss on the bottom of the basket so that the pieces overlap slightly. Arrange for some of the larger pieces to curve upward toward the sides of the frame so that a 2-inch layer of potting soil can be added (figure A).

Figure A

3. Add the first layer of plants. To add a plant, choose a young trailing variety you have separated from a six-pack. Working from the outside of the basket, poke the roots between the wire slats so that they rest on top of the first layer of potting soil.

4. Add several plants at this level, spacing them evenly around the sides of the basket. Build up more moss around the sides and add a second layer of potting soil. The plants from the first layer now have their roots buried under this second layer of soil (figure B).

5. Add more plants to the second layer, working from the outside and poking their roots between the wires. Fill in

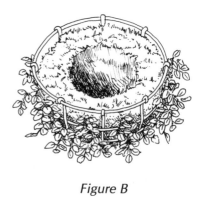

Figure B

with more moss along the sides of the basket as you discover spots where the potting soil is leaking out. Use your largest plants and those with a more upright growth habit for filling in the top level.

6. Finish off the top of the basket by wrapping the moss around the rim and adding a final layer of soil. Be sure to leave at least an inch of space between the soil and the top of the basket for the plants to collect water (figure C).

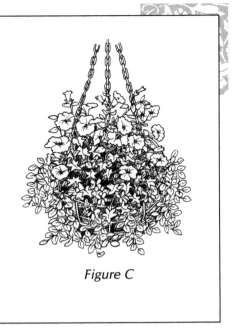

Figure C

potted planters so the standing pots can collect the overflow of water. If you live where summer water restrictions are a fact of life, this type of arrangement allows you to recycle your water and fertilizer at the same time.

❖ Coordinate the style or color of your porch containers with the color of your front door. Matching flower pots with the color of your house trim is a classic entry scene, and painting them is the easiest way to do this. If you look at photographs of front doors in European towns and villages, you'll notice how often the doors, shutters, window boxes, and flowerpots are painted the same color. Paint is a great way to make an odd collection of containers look like a set.

WINDOW BOXES

Add a window box to your porch-level windows. Not only can a window box be painted a trim color to add instant impact, but flowers growing at sill level can be enjoyed both inside and out. A window box adds instant charm to traditional homes and gives needed character to simple houses with plain facades.

ADDING A WINDOW BOX

If you choose to add a window box near the front entry of your home, plan to make the depth at least 6 inches. This way, you can take a wonderful shortcut whenever the box needs flowers: Just purchase plants in bloom from a greenhouse and set them right in the window box, pot and all. Even if you plan to grow flowers from seed, don't plant them directly into the soil of the window box: Grow the seedlings in plastic pots that can be set in the box. This makes it easy to rotate spring, summer, and fall bloomers for continuous color. Use Styrofoam pellets as drainage material in the bottom of the window box and to adjust the height of the flowerpots. Hide the rims of the plastic pots with a covering of bark chips or of moss.

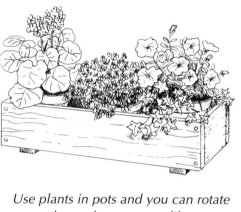

Use plants in pots and you can rotate them whenever you like.

Building a window box is easy. Sturdy outdoor brackets from a hardware store or home center are the secret shortcut to quick window box construction. Here are some tips for building a window box:

❖ The width of the brackets tells you how wide to build the box (usually between 6 and 10 inches).

❖ If you build your own rectangular box, use brass screws to secure the pieces together. Screws give more stability, and brass won't rust.

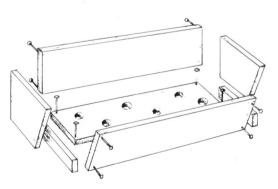

It's easy to make a window box.

❖ If you use a wood preservative (not necessary if you choose redwood or cedar), avoid creosote, which is toxic.

❖ Don't forget to paint or stain the window box to match the trim on your house.

Winter Window Box Color

Nothing is as dismal as an empty window box or one filled with frozen plants. After the first hard frost kills the fall flower display, replace the pots of flowers with boughs of holly or cedar. There's no need to pot these evergreens. Just snip off branch tips from your shrubs and arrange them in a fan shape in your boxes. Long ivy strands can also do winter duty.

THE FRONT DOOR

Those of us who are garden fanatics often ignore such trivial concerns as a weather-beaten door or a house in need of a paint job. It's time to face the peeling varnish, dirt-stained doorknobs, and dog scratches. Even a showcase garden can't camouflage a house in need of repair.

Architects talk about landscaping merely as the gilded frame for a picture-perfect house, whereas gardeners think of the house as a necessary structure that takes ground area from their precious garden space. Let's compromise and suggest that the front garden and the house it adorns are mutually necessary. Even if all you want to do is dig in the dirt, force yourself to spend some energy on cosmetic improvements to the front of the house. If houses are your first love, learn to appreciate and cultivate plant life and exterior designs that show off your beautiful building. These tips toward better doorways are especially important if you need a quick shortcut to improve the appearance of your house while you wait for the garden of your dreams to take form.

Paint the Door

Painting the front door a vibrant color is a tradition that hasn't caught on in the United States the way it has in Europe. If you've never thought of livening up your entrance with a paint job, consider these points:

❖ Most front doors are small enough to handle the intensity of an accent color.

❖ It takes only a few hours to repaint or change the color of a door if you don't like what you've done.

❖ Many doorways are protected from the weather by a roof overhang, so the paint job will last for a number of years.

The right type of paint and proper prepainting preparation information is as close as the nearest hardware store. Ask to talk with an experienced paint professional, and you'll get gallons of free advice on everything from the best type of brush to use to the best time of day to paint your door.

Paint can be used to improve other parts of your entry design as well. Cement steps and even brickwork can be painted to hide years of age and neglect. Plants stand out and look healthier against a fresh, clean backdrop.

If you still think spending time and money on your front door area is bothersome, remember that visitors have to stand and wait until you answer your door and are a captive audience for your doorway displays of drama. Color is the quickest way to change the look of a doorway area.

I found a good example of how a bucket of paint and a few pots of flowers improved a front landscape in a neighborhood of older homes that I drive through frequently. The older house I'm thinking of was recently sold, and the new owners wanted to improve the front yard quickly. The transformation seemed to happen overnight (they later admitted it took a weekend) and cost them only a can of red enamel paint. Not only did they paint the front door of their old gray house a fire engine red, but they complemented the paint job with a freshly painted bright red wagon that their children had outgrown. Into the wagon went an odd assortment of containers planted with shade-loving white impatiens. The family also trimmed around the doorbell and painted the nearby metal house numbers red as a finishing touch.

Everyone who passed this home could see from the curb how quickly the property was being improved, and guests couldn't help but feel a welcoming excitement as they stood in front of a brilliant red door. It's December as I write this, and I've noticed that the owners have outlined the red door with a simple strand of white lights. A traditional evergreen wreath with a scarlet bow gives this once-neglected house a much-loved look, even though the lawn is still in need of renovation and the shrubbery is still overgrown. (They'll get to that in the spring.) Call it a coincidence if you like, but three more houses on that block are now also sprouting bright new trim colors and blooming with pots of flowers on the front stoop.

Red is such a strong color that it may not appeal to every homeowner or match every house style. Other accent colors popular in different parts of the United States are bright teal, warm yellow, soft peach, and, of course, shiny black.

Most of us think of painting our front door to match the color that is used around the windows and trim of the house, which is usually a few shades darker or lighter than the neutral color of the house. Even a color scheme as safe and traditional as light gray and dark gray can be livened up with a painted porch accent.

There sits in our town a two-story, boxy house with a traditional gray-and-white color scheme. The front porch is nothing more than a small square of cement, but sitting in one corner is a tiny wooden wheelbarrow just big enough to hold a few 4-inch pots of pansies. The wheelbarrow is painted the same gray-blue color as the shutters, front door, and trim on this traditional house. In this case, instead of a dramatic color like red, a more subtle color that blends with the house was used to liven up the entry. A fresh coat of darker gray paint on the door did wonders, but it is the simple accent of the matching painted wheelbarrow filled with

A simple accent can make an entry inviting.

flowers that made this entire scene traditional but whimsical, warm, and inviting. The tip here is to add more color by using an accent piece and matching it with paint to the traditional, Colonial feel of the architecture.

Let me confess right now that my own front door is plain brown wood. My excuse for this dull door is that it is only a few years old, the wood finish is still in great shape, and I haven't the heart to sand off a perfectly good finish and apply paint in some wild and lively color. Actually, I need to start now if, in a few more years, I am to convince my husband, Joe, that a perfectly good wood door would look even better with a coat of shiny enamel paint. As soon as the door shows signs of weathering, I'll make my move with the paintbrush.

I've even figured out how to get my color-conservative man to go for a bright red or emerald green entryway. I'm going to start campaigning for a shocking pink or a deep purple paint job on our front door. After days of paint chips and color tests, Joe will recoil in horror at the thought that I'm serious and he could actually come home to a passionate purple passageway. This is when I'll offer a compromise. I'll generously give up my original desire for pink or purple (the wild colors he thinks I'm torn between) and offer to go with boring bright red or traditional emerald green instead. Joe will be so relieved that he'll probably buy the paint for the door himself.

Of course, if he doesn't offer to do the painting, I'll just go ahead and start the project on a Saturday when he's home playing with his power tools. A paintbrush doesn't attract my husband the way noisy, powerful gadgets do (the sound of a chain saw gets his blood pumping), but watching me with a paintbrush in hand is enough to drive my neat-and-tidy husband into a nervous drip-watcher. He'll hover anxiously around to make sure I spread enough newspaper to protect the cement porch (he loves cement), and then once he realizes I'm really going to dip my paintbrush in the paint, drip anxiety will overcome him and he'll beg me to let him paint. That will be just fine with me, because one of the most effective home improvement shortcuts you can take is to convince somebody else to carry out the labor of your great ideas.

Other Door Treatments

If you and your family can't agree on a lively accent color for your front door, or if painting just doesn't seem appropriate to your style of house, there are other ways to dress up the doorway. Consider these shortcuts to dress up a dismal front door:

❖ New molding around the door frame

❖ New railing around the porch

❖ A dramatic light fixture, either wall- or ceiling-mounted

❖ A personalized door knocker

Another door-brightening idea is to buy a brass kickplate (available at hardware and home improvement stores). A kickplate is the shiny rectangle of brass that is used on the bottom one-fourth of a door to protect it when somebody kicks the door open. Once you have spent the time and money attaching a kickplate to your front door, you won't dare allow anyone to kick it and scuff up that shiny brass. A better name for these shiny embellishments would be **anti**kickplates.

An interesting thing about kickplates (besides their name) is how fashionable they are becoming in certain neighborhoods. You don't need a traditional Colonial home to enjoy a shiny brass kickplate, doorknob, and door knocker. Although more expensive homes are more likely to invest in such a classy door accent, I have noticed an outbreak of kickplates in more modest neighborhoods. One couple proudly proclaimed themselves the source of the fad in their development. As often happens, once one energetic family begins to improve the front of their home, others in the neighborhood look at their own humdrum exteriors with new eyes. It's not, "Let's keep up with the Joneses," but rather, "Let's reward the Joneses." You get to look at their nicely tended front yard, so why not generate a little pride in the neighborhood and paint, pot, and plant up your front yard for them to admire?

Adding front door color, pots of flowers, or a kickplate won't work for every entryway. Some of you may have no affection for painting or may have a front stoop hidden from view with no room for even one little pot of plants. Some of you, like my husband, who loves only vanilla ice cream and solid-colored bedspreads, can't handle the intensity of carnival colors. There's another way to enlarge the welcome to your home — by widening the path to your front door.

Widening the Walkway

One of the first things I usually change when I'm hired to improve a landscape is the path that goes from the driveway to the front door. Most of the people for whom I do garden designs don't need a set of blueprint designs drawn to scale, they just want a few landscape improvement ideas and the names of plants that won't die. These are busy people, so low maintenance and a modest budget are important when they consider any landscaping project. Widening the path that ushers visitors to the front entry is an improvement that most homeowners can accomplish themselves in a short period of time and on a limited budget. The result is a front garden area more open and inviting and, most important, more practical than the typical narrow walkway that many homeowners are stuck with. Here are a few ideas for opening up the walk to your entry:

❖ Widening your walkway can be as simple as adding bricks or paving stones to the borders of the cement path already in place. Lay the new border at the same level as the original path.

❖ A good pruning of overgrown shrubs can work miracles. Clear out those overgrown shrubs unless you're partial to cave dwelling or need to camouflage your residence for military maneuvers.

Add bricks to widen your walkway.

❖ Adding gravel to one or both sides of the pathway is another quick way to eliminate the feeling that you're navigating on a tightrope. Sinking stepping-stones or cement pavers into the gravel border is even better because you then have the perfect spot for displaying pots of flowers.

❖ A front yard courtyard can be added to any house style, not just the Mediterranean/desert style that often makes use of the front courtyard entrance.

ADD A COURTYARD

There are three basic variations of the front yard courtyard that I often use to widen the entryway and dress up a typical front yard — and they all follow the path of least resistance. The arrangement of the existing path and driveway (or lack thereof) determines which courtyard design is easiest for a homeowner to add to her or his front landscape.

❖ Side driveway with a straight L-shaped path to the front door. This involves adding a courtyard straight out from the front door. The entire path can also be widened so that there is a patio to the front door instead of a narrow pathway.

❖ Side driveway with a curving path to the front door. This leaves an awkward section of garden sandwiched between the house and the pathway. It is often dark and shady if on the north or east side and hot and dry if heat is trapped in the alcove on the south or west side of the house. I like to turn the whole area into an outdoor room with a bench instead of a sofa, outdoor lighting rather than a reading lamp, and pots of flowers in place of end tables. Use a bit of ground cover to act as an area rug and frame any windows with planter boxes and shutters instead of curtains or drapes.

❖ Center walkway up the middle of the front lawn. The center path is widened to become a courtyard to pass through. It can also serve as a display or sitting area on the way to the door. This won't destroy the symmetry of a traditional home and will open up the view to the front door (freshly painted, of course). A sundial, birdbath, or other formal focal point can be used in this widened area instead of a bench if the space is limited.

❖ Courtyard entry of staggered rectangles of cement instead of the more traditional designs. This design complements contemporary homes or those with an Oriental influence.

HOW TO CONSTRUCT THE COURTYARD

The addition of a courtyard or front sitting area to your landscape may not seem like a shortcut at first, but it can be a weekend project — if you're a fast worker with a lot of luck. But most do-it-yourselfers have to break this job into steps that may take several weekends to complete.

The first weekend, get a bag of flour and use it like chalk to draw the size and shape of your proposed courtyard on the ground. You can also use string and stakes to mark the shape of the new area. Now, dig out the lawn or remove the plants from this section. Don't try to pour cement or fill in with a gravel surface the same day. (Something always goes wrong with every home improvement project, and I shall admit now that every idea presented in this book will take twice as long as you think it will.) Outlining a courtyard or widening a path will take four times as long as you've planned if you need to confer and compromise with a spouse about the size, shape, or materials used to construct this courtyard.

The second weekend of the courtyard project will probably break all records for horribly uncomfortable weather conditions because this is the weekend you have to spend outdoors raking in the gravel (have it delivered unless you want to break an axle), pouring cement, or laying brick. You will be so exhausted from the experience that you won't even feel like looking at your creation, let alone adding any finishing touches. Save that for the third weekend.

During the third and fourth weekends, you might complete the surface of the new courtyard, but factor in the possibility that the cement or gravel you ordered won't be delivered to the right address and that you'll run out of paving material, landscape timbers, or Band-aids. Give yourself another weekend or two to finish what started out to be a simple weekend project.

Before you give up, think it's too much bother, and stop reading about courtyard materials and construction techniques, consider this: So, it takes you more than a month of weekends to widen your entry with a courtyard. That same month is going to pass by anyway, and you might as well devote your free time to building something lasting that will improve your property value, delight your neighbors, welcome your guests, and keep you from only reading about landscape improvements. The maintenance on a courtyard area is a lot less time-consuming than the care required to tend a lawn or whatever plants the courtyard is replacing. A front courtyard can give you a place to sit and to show off flowers, and, most important, it can transform the look of your front garden from boring to beautiful.

There are various types of courtyards. Following are some examples.

Gravel or Cedar Chips

These materials are laid on a level surface and bordered with large stones or landscape timbers. This casual, easy-to-construct style works best with a woodland, country, or contemporary garden style. Use rocks or bricks to form the outline instead of timbers if you want a free-form or oval look. Use small-pebble gravel and landscape timbers in a diamond or an octagonal pattern for a more formal look. To discourage weeds, line the surface with landscape fabric before filling in with gravel or wood chips.

Brick or Cement Pavers

This type of surface needs a sand base at least 2 to 3 inches deep to keep the freezing and thawing of the soil from heaving up the bricks. You can sweep dry sand into the cracks between bricks or pavers, or you can add dry mortar, water it down, and wait for the cement to set the surface. Find a supplier of bricks or pavers in your area and ask these professionals for more specific installation information. Each climate zone has its own construction requirements for a dry-laid brick or paver surface.

GREAT GARDENS FOR FRONT YARD COURTYARDS

Plants that border your courtyard or the path to your front door will be observed up close. They also need a more upright and formal growth pattern to keep them from spilling over and blocking the garden path. Below are some well-behaved plants that complement the courtyard look:

Rose Garden

Use tree roses as accents at the entry to a courtyard and low-growing floribunda shrub roses to make a blooming hedge. Examples of floribundas are 'Fairy' in pink, 'Europeana' in red, and 'Iceberg' in white.

Fragrance Garden

A front yard that smells good is as enjoyable as a front yard that looks good. You can frame your front yard courtyard with fragrance if you choose compact blooming shrubs such as rock daphne *(Daphne odora);* spring-blooming bulbs that perfume the air; and summer annuals that smell as good as they look. Try Asiatic lilies; bearded iris varieties with heavy fragrance, such as 'Victoria Falls'; flowering tobacco *(Nicotiana alata);* fragrant petunias, such as the purple-veined 'Sugar Daddy'; hyacinths and sweet violets *(Viola odorata);* and sweet alyssum *(Lobularia maritima)*.

Herbal Garden

Border your courtyard and path to the front door with low, shrubby herbs, such as lavender cotton *(Santolina chamaecyparissus)*, English lavender *(Lavandula angustifolia)*, or germander *(Teucrium chamaedrys)*. In mild climates, the germander and santolina remain evergreen throughout the winter. These plants can be trimmed into tidy hedges. Add a few favorite herbs for cooking, such as parsley, oregano, and basil, and you'll have a cook's welcome to your entry. Low-growing thyme, especially the dependable woolly thyme *(Thymus pseudolanuginosus)*, can be used between stepping-stones or pavers in an herbal courtyard. It's easy to make an herbal knot garden (see illustration), but if you don't have the time to maintain one, you can simply use its design as inspiration.

Making an Herbal Knot Garden

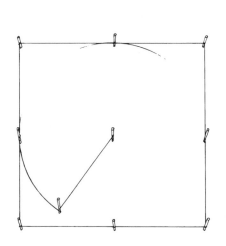

Step 1. Use pegs to mark the corners and side midpoints of the square. Tie string to the opposite-corner pegs to find the square's center.

Step 2. Tie string and a peg to the center peg and draw a circle.

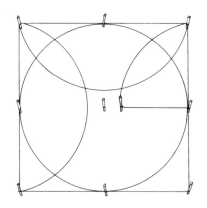

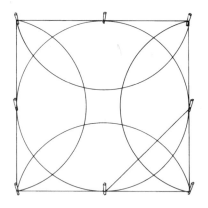

Step 3. Tie string and a peg to the midpoint pegs and draw semicircles on all four sides.

Step 4. Draw a diamond by stretching string between the four midpoints.

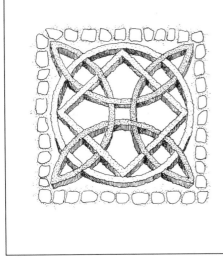

Step 5. Plant the circle, diamond, and semicircles with bushy herbs in contrasting colors (for example, lavender, gray santolina, and green santolina).

Cement or Exposed Aggregate

This is the lowest-maintenance type of courtyard because weeds can't grow. However, working with cement takes more skill than using the other materials. If you decide to hire this project out to professionals (hiring professionals is a wonderful but expensive shortcut), you can add a personal touch by asking that a brick border, exposed aggregate, or polished stones be set into the wet cement. You might even have the patience to decorate the surface with leaf imprints while the finish dries.

The most personal path I've ever had the pleasure of walking on was created by a family who added not only the handprints of their children and the dates but also a metal knitting needle, random coins, footsteps, and paw prints from their pets. The embellishments were kept to the edges of the walkway, and the wild collection of imprints looked like a border of modern art that matched up nicely with their contemporary house and landscape.

Are knitting needles and paw prints in the cement a little too wild for you? How about just spelling out the house number with pebbles or setting numbered tiles into the path to announce the address? If you have a set of cement stairs that leads to the front door, why not use a cement tile adhesive and decorate the risers of those steps with tile artwork or your house numbers?

Outlining the lawn or courtyard area with professionally poured cement curbing has become accessible to the average homeowner with the development of portable curbing machines. (Check in the telephone book under

Cement to find a company that provides this service in your area.) A house in our neighborhood sports a personalized cement curb: The owner used smooth rocks and laid them into the wet cement to form a highly textured cobblestone look. You can do the same thing to a cement pathway, using whatever size and shape of stone predominate in your yard.

Widen your horizons about what's acceptable material for a pathway when you widen the walk, and welcome your guests to a very personal and unique front entry garden.

Putting Your Personality on the Porch

A garden accent is a little extra such as a birdbath, a sundial, a bench, or an arch. Garden focal points and accent pieces are more fully addressed in Chapter 4, but right now we need to consider how to dress up your entry easily with a porch accent. The preceding examples showed how a pot of flowers, a red wagon, or a miniature wheelbarrow on a porch can add to the make-over. Just think of an accent as the little thing that adds a lot.

When you make choices about dressing up your front entryway, you should consider your landscape style and personality. Following are examples of doorway accents that fit into the five major landscape styles. Of course, your own imagination will be fertile and ripe with the seeds of inspiration after reading this list. So, go ahead and reject every idea presented here in a marvelously independent move toward personal expression, and use your own ideas. The introduction to your home will never again lack the character and personality of those living inside. These doorway accents have been grouped according to the garden styles they most often represent. If you haven't yet decided your house or garden style, review Chapter 1 or pick any accent ideas that appeal to you and go from there.

FORMAL/ESTATE STYLE

- Brass door knocker and brass kickplate
- Urn-style container filled with ivy or geraniums
- Wrought-iron planters and stair railing (painted to match)
- Forged iron or formal outdoor furniture on the porch
- Stone lions guarding the entrance
- Cast concrete planters set on pedestals

- Matched set of hanging moss baskets or collection of hanging baskets, all filled with identical flowers and spaced evenly apart on the porch
- **Colors:** Solid and traditional colors such as red and white are very formal. Tree roses and geraniums in any solid color give a formal feeling. The estate look favors solid blocks of color over mixed plantings, so fill your porch containers with only one or two kinds of flowers. White flowers cascading over the edges of pots look crisp and formal, so use white lobelia and sweet alyssum as a companion to your potted geraniums and marigolds. For spring color, white and red tulips, either potted or in nearby display beds, look especially regal. The front doors can be painted emerald green, shiny black, or bright red. Several coats of paint with a shiny finish give doors that deep, rich look that estates are so famous for.

COUNTRY/COTTAGE STYLE

- Wide-brimmed straw hat on the door
- Watering can set on the porch or used as a planter
- Half-basket or bicycle basket on the door for letters
- Wicker furniture or wicker plant stands on the porch
- Stone animals sitting about like the perfect pets that they are
- Wood or wicker porch swing
- **Colors:** Pastel flowers in muted tones of lavender, pink, and blue look great with the casual look of country. Trailing lobelia, ruffled petunias, and miniature roses are favorites for porch containers. Blue, dusty rose, and clay red are traditional country colors for the front door.

CONTEMPORARY/ORIENTAL STYLE

- Stone or iron outdoor sculpture or any artwork with clean lines
- Textured surface of pathway and walls, such as exposed aggregate cement
- Stone pagoda or lantern
- Dish- or bowl-shaped planters made from exposed aggregate
- Woven straw mat used as a wall hanging or doormat

- ◆ Lots of space and a simple, uncluttered entryway
- ◆ Bonsai specimens in shallow planters or beautifully shaped specimen plants in containers
- ◆ Trees and shrubs with a contemporary look that adapt well to porch container culture include *Camellia sasanqua* (for a sprawling form), juniper (*Juniperus chinensis* 'San Jose' and 'Torulosa' are slow growing and easy to keep trimmed for a bonsai look; low-growing junipers such as *Juniperus horizontalis* 'Wiltonii' and 'Bar Harbor' adapt to the pot-bound life by spilling gracefully over the edges of the container), and small-leaved maples such as the brilliant red Amur maple *(Acer ginnala)* and Japanese maple *(Acer palmatum)*.
- ◆ **Colors:** Stained wood and natural-looking surfaces have a more contemporary look than painted wood, although the shiny lacquered look of a red or black door gives a distinctive Oriental look.

NATURALISTIC/WOODLAND STYLE

- ◆ A pair of painted or whimsically decorated boots sitting on the porch
- ◆ Twig furniture and stained wooden planters
- ◆ Pinecone wreath or braided straw wreath on the door
- ◆ Child's wheelbarrow, tractor, or wooden chair used as a plant holder
- ◆ Rusty tools or machine parts nailed to the wall as a display
- ◆ Wooden milk crates or tool tote used as planters
- ◆ Rustic birdhouse, bird feeder, or wind chimes hanging from the eaves
- ◆ Wooden poles or wood carvings
- ◆ **Colors:** The green of foliage plants, especially ferns, looks at home on the front porch of a log cabin, an A-frame house, or another rustic style of architecture. Warm colors from casual flowers such as orange and gold nasturtiums and yellow marigolds make a nice contrast to stained wood siding. Nasturtiums spilling from recycled containers make an inexpensive color spot. For the front door, consider dark green or terra-cotta, two of the earth tones that complement a rustic wood exterior.

MEDITERRANEAN/DESERT STYLE

- Stoneware and hand-painted pottery
- Tile surfaces or tile-decorated planters
- Worn wooden tools displayed on the wall
- Heavy wood furniture on the porch
- Wrought-iron plant stands
- Rope, blankets, leather goods, and other cowboy artifacts displayed on the wall
- Terra-cotta pots: Container gardens are easy to care for and rich in texture if planted with succulents such as hen and chickens *(Sempervivum tectorum)*, living stones *(Lithops)*, and members of the jade family *(Crassula)*. Heat-tolerant hanging plants include burro's tail *(Sedum morganianum)* and Christmas cactus *(Schlumbergera bridgesii)*. If you don't live in a frost-free area, be sure to bring these tender plants indoors for the winter.
- **Colors:** Hot, bright colors stand out against whitewashed or plaster walls, so blooming plants in reds, yellows, oranges, and hot pinks look great. Plants with gray foliage also look at home in a desert setting, so consider santolina, French lavender *(Lavandula dentata)*, and Russian sage *(Perovskia atriplicifolia)* for potted herbs or shrubby doorway plantings. Front doors are usually wood-stained a deep brown or a bleached-out color.

Protecting and Illuminating the Scene

If you're sadly shaking your head at the entryway accents mentioned earlier because you're a city dweller who thinks of theft first and design second, keep reading. Those of us who live in small towns realize that, in many neighborhoods, you can't be casual about displaying anything outdoors that is not rooted in or nailed down. To avoid the violation of the thieving rascals that may rob your porch under cover of darkness, take these security measures:

- Install a motion-detector porch light. These inexpensive gadgets flip on a bright light as soon as movement in the area is detected.

- Install a welcome mat that buzzes or rings when stepped on, like the ones shops use to announce the arrival of a customer.

❖ Use nails or glue on your lightweight accents and wire or screws to secure other pieces. The clay pots at the end of our driveway are secured with a piece of wire that runs through the drainage hole at the bottom of the pot and then up and over the edge, making a loop that is fastened to the cement footings of our brick wall. The wire is hardly noticeable until you try to lift the heavy pots. Glue, nails, and wire do wonders to keep nonprofessional thieves honest by making theft more difficult.

❖ Accept that theft and vandalism have been around as long as humankind. I've heard of newly landscaped yards totally barren of plants after a single overnight raid, well-established trees dug and sold on the green market, pots of geraniums and fuchsia baskets lifted in broad daylight, and a plastic baby Jesus stolen from an outdoor nativity set. Now that you've imagined the worst, consider all the trees, flowers, shrubs, and garden accents that stay just where they've been put. The odds are in your favor. Robbers and thieves may be so enchanted with your newly improved front landscape that even they won't have the heart to destroy the lovely scene.

❖ One last security measure you should take is to invest in good lighting. The lighting you use can do more than just protect your property. The next section explains how proper lighting can turn a common front yard into a moonlit wonderland.

LIGHT YOUR WAY TO A SHOWCASE GARDEN

The one improvement that will guide your guests to the doorway, make your home more secure, and illuminate the whole idea about more exciting entrances is outdoor lighting. If you have any doubts about the level of showmanship that can go into outdoor lighting, make a twilight visit to one of the internationally known show gardens. The Butchart Gardens and Minter Gardens are two in the Pacific Northwest that are lit up at night for a totally different viewing experience.

Although most homeowners won't go to the twinkling excess that these gardens display, here are a few lighting secrets that can add drama to your own nightscape:

❖ Low-voltage or solar-powered footlights can be very effective, but for an even shorter route to a brighter doorway, replace your old bulb with a higher-voltage one or clean the dead insects and dust off the bulb you have. You can also repaint, repair, or replace any wall-mounted lighting units and get a new post or pillar for the freestanding light in your front yard.

❖ Border a walkway with a string of low-voltage lights at ground level. It will look similar to the aisle at a movie theater.

❖ Light up the stairway with the same low-voltage lights in the risers. Home centers sell special lights just for this spot.

❖ Use a spotlight to focus on the house numbers. (The use of a spotlight to showcase plants is discussed in Chapter 5.)

❖ Spotlight the front door or the porch focal point with a can spotlight hidden in the shrubbery.

Most-Asked Questions about Entryways

Q. *Help! My front entryway faces west, and the hot afternoon sun cooks the plants I try to grow in hanging baskets. I can usually keep ivy geraniums alive for a few months, but by midsummer the leaves are yellow and the plant has stopped blooming. I won't even mention the fuchsia baskets and hanging impatiens that have died over the years. I am almost desperate enough to hang out baskets of fake flowers.*

A. Cool down and avoid the artificial life forms. Even the best imitation flowers won't look realistic for long because they fade horribly in the sun. What you need is to be rescued by the plants of steel. Ivy geraniums and many other blooming annuals such as lobelia and flowering tobacco *(Nicotiana)* love the sun but can't take the heat that collects in southern or western entryways. Choose super-tough, heat-tolerant flowers for your porch such as marigolds (dwarf marigolds are great for hanging baskets), zonal geraniums *(Pelargonium X hortorum)*, gazania daisies, portulaca, and salvia. Remember to water often during warm weather. Potted plants may even need water twice a day.

Q. *I have a long, narrow entry garden in deep shade. The entrance to my condominium is on the shady, north side that is further darkened by a*

SUREFIRE SHORTCUTS

❖ Instantly hide the cracked or broken concrete leading to your front door with a covering of outdoor carpet. You might also splurge on a large, colorful welcome mat to cover any not-so-welcoming surface.

❖ If you have wrought-iron railings next to your steps, paint them a lively trim color, and use the same paint on your house numbers and porch light fixtures.

❖ Use a bit of paint to trim the rim of your clay pots. An unrelated group of containers can be made to look like a set by adding a single band of coordinating paint.

❖ Decorate your door and entry garden for the holidays.

❖ Change your porch accents with each of the four seasons (dried cornstalks or squash for fall, a wreath or basket of cones for winter, potted bulbs for spring, and pots of annuals or hanging baskets of flowers for summer).

❖ Stencil a simple design on the front of window boxes or around the door frame.

❖ Keep all permanent outdoor containers filled with greenery, even during the winter months. Arrange cut holly and evergreen boughs in your empty window boxes and porch containers.

❖ Upgrade your exterior light fixtures.

❖ Add a child-sized chair or a tiny bench to a small porch. Use any small accents as plant stands for your containers of seasonal flowers.

❖ If boots and shoes collect on your porch, add a large hamper or basket to corral them in.

❖ Get a new mailbox if yours is looking sad. Paint it a custom color or liven it up with a whimsical design and brighten the mail carrier's route.

❖ Choose a container for the porch just large enough to hold the 6-inch plastic pots in which florists grow flowering plants. Even if you don't have a green thumb, you can rotate pots of blooming plants in the porch container and replace them with newly budded plants as needed.

tall building next door. Any plants I try to grow end up looking stretched out and weak as they reach for the sun. My planting area is 10 feet long but only 8 inches wide and sandwiched between the side of the building and the cement path that leads to the door.

A. There are plenty of plants besides mushrooms and mosses that tolerate deep shade. First, consider painting the walls of your "cave" white to reflect as much light as possible. Next, try hanging baskets of flowers suspended from the eaves or wall brackets. Planters up in the air get more light than those at ground level. Use a covering of white rocks or light-colored gravel to cover the ground in your long, narrow planting bed. Put your plant collection in pots sitting on top of this gravel base. This maneuver breaks up the tunnel vision that narrow walkways cause.

For the shade-loving flowering plants, the best choice is undoubtedly impatiens. The variety 'Blitz' was bred for hanging baskets, and the aptly named 'Shady Lady' series is a profuse bloomer. Plants with colorful foliage, such as coleus (especially the compact "carefree coleus" series) and caladium, also add color without blossoms.

Other annual flowers that bloom in light shade include lobelia, tuberous and fibrous begonia, forget-me-not, ageratum, browallia, and fuchsia. You can also try replacing your porch light with a grow light and rotating your potted plants to a brighter location every week or so when they become leggy.

Q. *Our house sits back from the road down a curving driveway, and the mailbox is the only thing our neighbors see from the street. I would like to landscape around the mailbox with plants that have color year-round but don't demand too much care.*

A. For special delivery of a carefree flower garden, get the color by planting bulbs and bushes. Flowering shrubs and bulbs that naturalize give you the most color for the least amount of care. Start with a background of early-blooming shrubs, as well as those with fall color. Use bulbs for spring and summer color.

One of the earliest blooming shrubs is flowering almond (*Prunus glandulosa* 'Sinensis'), followed by crocuses and daffodils for early-spring color. Plant the later-blooming tulips and bearded irises in front of the early bulbs so that they'll screen out the fading foliage of the early bloomers. Allow a clematis, such as *Clematis* x *Jackmanii*, to scramble up the pole that holds the mailbox, then group summer bloomers down low in front of your mailbox garden. Cranesbill geranium *(Geranium endressii)* is a mounded, undemanding plant that blooms all summer and shades the roots of the clematis. For shots of more summer color and fragrance, plant bulbs of Asiatic lilies, daylilies, and lily of the Nile *(Agapanthus africanus)*. End the bulb color display with autumn-blooming crocus *(Crocus speciosus)*.

Use more shrubs in the background for fall and winter color. The dwarf burning bush *(Euonymus alata* 'Compacta') is brilliant in autumn, and members of the cotoneaster or yew family give evergreen winter color accented with brightly colored berries.

Chapter Summary

❖ Use color to call attention to your front entryway. Front doors and pots can be painted the same accent color, or touches of tile or hanging plants can quickly add a dose of color near the entrance.

❖ Widen the walk to your front door, making the whole yard seem more inviting. The addition of gravel or stepping-stones alongside an established path is an easy way to stretch a walkway's width. This may even give you enough space for setting out potted plants next to the path.

❖ Prune back or pull out the overgrown shrubbery around paths and doors.

❖ Consider adding a front yard courtyard to your landscape. This can be a private area screened from the public or a formal courtyard installed to open up and properly present a formal front door.

❖ Choose porch furniture and doorway accents to coordinate with the general style of your house, landscape, and personality. Give them the same thought as you would indoor furniture and artwork.

❖ Add nighttime sparkle with low-voltage lighting and dramatically highlight accents with spotlighting. This is especially important if you often have evening guests.

CHAPTER 3

Add a Garden Vista: The Shortcut to a Great View

SHORTCUT:

Create a pleasant scene or vista in your garden and call attention to it by leading the eye with a pathway, open space, or repetition of color and form.

Once you've improved the front entry area, it's time to widen your focus and pay attention to the view from porch or curbside. Although the front entry garden is enjoyed up close as the foreground to your house, the rest of the landscape is viewed from a distance as the background. This chapter focuses on arranging plants to create a scenic backdrop for your showcase garden.

To get you started on creating a scenic landscape, imagine the most beautiful garden in the world. Now, imagine yourself setting up a camera or an easel to capture this vision. You would probably have a pathway in view. Whether it's a country/cottage style you crave, with a flagstone path through foxgloves, or a formal/estate design with brick walkways bordered with roses, all great garden scenes lead somewhere. There's a reason for this: when your eye is led down a path toward a distant focal point, the view is satisfying. The creation of a successful garden scene is as simple as pleasing the eye.

You don't need a lot of property or a waterfront lot to take advantage of a great outdoor view. The secret to a well-designed landscape with an appealing vista is to create your own pleasing scene and then direct the eye toward it. Any piece of property, no matter how small, can boast of a garden vista.

Don't panic if you're barely familiar with violets and haven't even heard of a vista. This chapter and the entire book is intended to be beginner-friendly. A vista is just a classy-sounding word that means you have a background and a foreground in your landscape. Expensive and educated landscape architects love to create vistas, talk about vistas, and visit vistas. It's time everyone had a vista for his or her own backyard — and front yard, too.

If you'd like to throw the word *vista* around just to impress friends and neighbors, go ahead: You'll be in good company. For centuries, garden designers have been earning prestige and money by adding vistas to the landscapes of the rich and the royal. These successful landscape designers have been quick to add vistas when commissioned by royalty for two reasons: First, to give the royal eye a beautiful background to view, and second, to have an excuse to move a lot of earth, spend a lot of time, and charge a lot of money.

The famous 18th-century landscape designers were fond of telling rich landowners that their manor estates lacked backgrounds and good views. They would convince their status-conscious clients to move hillsides, to add valleys and lakes, and even to create tiny villages, Roman ruins, and castle towers — just to hold and direct the eye over the vastness of the client's property.

You, however, should add a vista to your landscape for these reasons: First, to give your own eyes someplace nice to view, and second, to save yourself lots of money, lots of time, and lots of work.

On a small scale, you can sneak by with less plant material in the rest of the yard if you plan for a pleasant view (or vista) on which the eye can focus. You more or less group all the good stuff in a single area and direct attention toward this showcase section of the yard.

As an example of how budget-conscious gardeners can use a vista to conserve plant material, consider using inexpensive junipers or ground cover plants along the sides of a lawn and then splurging on a lovely red lace-leaved maple or majestic weeping Atlantic cedar as the focal point of the planting bed. By using large boulders or a mound of earth to draw more attention to the focal point plant, you can get away with using more common and less expensive plants in the rest of the area.

Adapting the vista idea to a small piece of property adds depth to a shallow lot and helps focus a long, narrow lot. A cluttered yard looks more organized, and a sparse-looking new landscape can be given an anchor from which to grow just by giving the eye something to follow and a place to rest. This is yet another

USING OPTICAL ILLUSIONS
TO MAKE A SMALL YARD SEEM BIGGER

❖ Stagger the grade of the beds. An easy way to do this is to use landscape timbers or bricks around the different planting areas.

❖ Use small units of paving material such as bricks or cobblestones to make your paths and patios. Giant stepping-stones can dwarf a small yard. Adding texture to a cement path by choosing an exposed aggregate or stamped-on finish also enhances a narrow path or tiny patio.

❖ Add a berm or mound of soil to an open area of lawn to vary the level and block the view of the end of the garden. If the eye can't quite see the boundaries, there is the illusion that there's a lot more waiting out there.

❖ Block the view in a narrow yard with a screen planting or divider set at an angle. Whenever a bit of screening is set at an angle in a short lot, there is the illusion of more depth.

❖ If you have steps off a deck or up a garden path, widen them. Make your steps at least 2 feet wide; 3 or 4 feet wide is even better.

❖ Vary the height of your plant material to stagger the garden ceiling. You can make small trees appear taller by surrounding them with low, ground-hugging shrubbery. A good example of this is a young, 10-foot blireiana plum tree *(Prunus* x *blireiana)*, a lovely specimen tree with early pink blossoms and burgundy foliage, surrounded by three Blue Mat junipers *(Juniperus horizontalis)* at its base. Any viewer would guess the tree to be 5 or 6 feet taller than it actually is, especially if the entire planting is on a mound.

❖ Have a sunken lawn. Even the tiniest grassy area looks larger when it's several steps lower than the rest of the   plantings or pavement. If you don't have the luxury of hiring a bulldozer to lower your lawn, simply raise all the beds around it instead.

example of how optical illusions and organization can improve the landscape. You'll understand how this "vista vision" can change the look of a front yard by studying the following examples.

Place stepping-stones across the lawn that disappear behind shrubbery. This is one of the simplest ways to add a vista to a small and simple front yard. Garden writers and landscape designers often state that a pathway that disappears out of sight is necessary to give the garden a feeling of mystery. You'd have to have a pretty boring life to find a garden path mysterious! Unless a cloak and a dagger have been left at the bend in the path or a trail of blood has been spilled on the stepping-stones, a pathway that disappears around the corner of a house may be intriguing, thought provoking, or a curiosity, but I just can't bring myself to say it adds mystery.

Disappearing stepping-stones add depth to a small yard.

Add a path spur off the walkway to the front door and have it lead to a focal point. The pathway to your front door naturally leads the eye to the main entrance, which forces it to become the focal point of the entire yard. A path spur added to the front walkway can make your landscape more interesting and your yard appear much larger. Position a birdbath, a bench or a pot of flowers at the end of the spur, and the new view you've created expands the visual limits of the space.

A path spur leading to an accent creates visual interest.

Use a teardrop-shaped addition to expand the shape of your main flower bed. Many older homes sit high off the ground, and a circle of foundation plantings or squat evergreens is used to bring the ground and the house together. Extend the evergreen planting out toward the center of the yard by using a small tree or other focal point in the center of a teardrop-shaped addition. The eye follows the shape of the house and is drawn outward toward the garden by the extension of the bed. Use a repetition of plant material, such as a

A teardrop-shaped addition enhances your flower bed.

staggered planting of azaleas or shrub roses, or a line of large boulders or annual flowers to lead the eye toward the focal point plant.

Add an archway to the side of the house and position a focal point (a bench, for instance) so that it can be viewed through the archway. This illusion adds depth to a landscape. Any small house appears longer when an arch or gate is added to its side, and a house with a high roofline has a smoother transition to ground level with the addition of a lower structure.

A simple opening in the fence line can be just as effective as an arch to draw the eye toward the back of the property. It is the centering of a focal point through the opening that makes the greatest impression, not the size or shape of the arch. You can even omit the overhead arch and draw the eye with a pathway around the side of the house. Keep the pathway clear

An archway with a focal point beyond creates the illusion of depth.

of obstructing shrubbery so that the scene can gain depth by borrowing from the backyard view.

Create a clearing in the hedge or shrubbery that borders your lawn. Add a gravel floor and center a large pot or urn in this clearing. Now, as you look out over the expanse of lawn, a focal point stands out from all the plants. Your view has just been changed from a wall of greenery blocking the view to a backdrop of greenery highlighting it. Even mature, fully established shrub borders benefit from clearing and trimming. Tall evergreen borders of yew or mature hedges of boxwood can be sheared back a little at a time to form a niche or opening in the wall of green. Use this space to display an urn of annuals, a sundial on a pedestal, or a birdhouse on a pole, and suddenly, the lines formed from your hedge become the frame for a peaceful garden scene.

Are you starting to get the picture? A vista is simply a pleasant view. Your garden vista should lead the eye to a specific point with a series of stepping-stones, a path, an archway, or an expanse of lawn. The addition of a vista to your yard has all the requirements of a good shortcut to a showcase garden: it's quick, easy, and effective. And it all begins with the focal point.

Clearing a niche in shrubbery highlights an accent.

Using Trees to Create a Vista

A double row of trees, all of the same size and type, is often used to lead the eye toward a vista. The French even have a name for this arrangement — an allée. In the days of manors and huge estates, the long approach to the main house was often beautified with shade trees spaced evenly apart on either side of the drive. This created a narrow field of vision and made the big house at the end of the drive stand out majestically as the strong focal point of the vista.

You can enjoy the same result on a smaller scale by planting three to five evenly spaced flowering trees in a line across the length or width of your property. And, if you happen to have a long driveway, an allée is an especially effective way to show off your home.

Many communities have planted evenly spaced street trees all of one kind to bring shade and beauty to the neighborhood. It's a wonderful idea, but notice how your attention is directed to the view ahead, down the street, and away from the view along the sides of the street. Keep this in mind when adding an allée of trees to your own landscape. Whatever is behind or parallel to the line of trees will be ignored, and whatever is at the end — be it your front door, garage, or a planted berm — will become the focal point.

QUICK PRUNING TIP

If you want to have neat, sheared hedges, prune them back lightly three times a year: St. Patrick's Day, Mother's Day, and the 4th of July. You won't be left with unsightly pruning scars.

Plant an allée to create a vista.

Using Color to Create a Vista

Blooming flowers always catch the eye, and repetition of color naturally leads it. However, some colors carry more visual weight than others. Cool colors such as blue, lavender, and purple recede into the background, whereas warm colors such as red, orange, yellow, and hot pink advance or stand out. Armed

GREAT TREES FOR CREATING AN ALLÉE IN A SMALL YARD

The small trees recommended here are suitable for planting in a row across a front yard or beside a driveway because they are well mannered and attractive. These trees do not have invasive root systems that are prone to crack sidewalks and choke septic systems, and they boast of flowers or foliage that ensure a showplace look.

Flowering Dogwood

Lovely fall foliage and outstanding spring flowers make this a favorite tree of many homeowners, but in recent years disease problems of *Cornus florida* have put a blight on the dogwood's good name as well as its foliage. A more carefree choice is the Korean dogwood *(Cornus kousa)*, which blooms in early summer rather than spring. The Korean dogwood also has a shrubbier growth habit than *Cornus florida,* making it a better choice for informal landscapes such as those with a naturalistic, Oriental, or country style.

Flowering Cherry

In spring, when pink blossoms decorate the flowering cherry *(Prunus serrulata),* no scene could be more beautiful than an allée of these delicate-looking trees. It's no wonder the Japanese hold celebrations at cherry blossom time. To conserve even more space, plant the narrow-growing Sargent cherry *(Prunus sargentii)* or the columnar cherry *(Prunus sargentii* 'Columnaris'). These two varieties grow more upright, allowing closer spacing than the usual 15 to 20 feet apart recommended for blooming trees. If you favor an Oriental-style garden, promise yourself you'll plant at least one flowering cherry tree, and if you have room, plant a double row of these fairy-tale trees. It could very well be the most beautiful planting decision of your lifetime.

The flowering cherries do have one weakness that is sadly illustrated across the front yard of a farmhouse near our town. An impressive row of 25 flowering cherries was planted across the front and down the side of a 2-acre lot. A white post-and-rail fence outlined the property and ran alongside the evenly spaced planting. No shrubs distracted from the beauty of the trees, and there was a huge but well-maintained sweep of lawn. The trees were young little whips when set into the ground that first fall, but anticipation neverthe-less mounted as the neighborhood waited for spring and the pink burst of color. The cherry trees did not disappoint, and double clusters of pink blossoms popped from the bare branches.

The problem started only after both heavy rain and new foliage showered the trees. The lot sloped away from the house, dipping down gradually to a low spot. Drainage water and root rot collected in this far corner, leaving a spreading path of rotting foliage and dying trees. The healthier-looking trees were those closest to the house and on higher ground. The root system of cherry trees won't tolerate poor drainage and clay soils, and today more than half of those struggling trees are dead. May they rest in peace, and may you vow to give flowering cherries well-drained soil or a raised bed or berm to grow in.

Flowering Plum

The compact growth habit and early display of blossoms make flowering plums almost as popular as their cousins, the flowering cherries. The variety *Prunus* x *blireiana* is especially popular as a street tree, which means it works well bordering residential driveways. The most impressive allée of flowering plums I ever saw was a planting of blireiana plums interspaced with forsythia bushes. It was February, a time when the sky is gray and the garden grayer, but these trees were covered with pink blossoms at the same time the forsythias burst into glorious yellow bloom.

A row of flowering plums and forsythias can maintain a formal look with an annual pruning to keep them from sprawling. If you prune right after New Year's Day, any wild branches that you tame with the pruning shears can be brought indoors and forced into bloom. Pruning these two companions will become a January tradition to look forward to.

Other trees that make a great chorus line, even though they lack the song-and-dance routine of the preceding blossoming trio, include *Ginkgo biloba*, Amur maple *(Acer ginnala)*, Japanese maple *(Acer palmatum)*, birch, redbud *(Cercis)*, some palms, and evergreens with an upright, columnar shape, such as 'Pyramidalis' arborvitae.

with this information, you can plant a flower garden with more depth by arranging for cool blues and lavender to be in the distance and hot colors to be up close or in front of a border. White and silver are neutral colors that can be used to unite the two color families.

In a mixed planting, you can lead the eye by using a staggered line of warm colors in a sea of cool blue tones. A classic spring planting is the combination of blue grape hyacinths splashed with 'Red Riding Hood' tulips. These two bulbs bloom at the same time, and the lower-growing blue hyacinths make the perfect backdrop for the taller red tulips. This beautiful example of companion planting is enhanced even more if the line of red tulips leads the eye to a focal point such as a small blooming shrub — a star magnolia, perhaps. The magnolia blooms at the same time as the early bulbs, and because it is larger than the bulb plants, it naturally stands out.

Allow me to introduce you to focal points. Any nonmoving object that catches and holds the eye because of its size, color, shape, or general beauty becomes a focal point. In the next chapter, I focus on focal points. Until then, just remember that flowering trees, birdbaths, sundials, and benches make good focal points, whereas junipers, ground covers, and romping dogs make lousy focal points.

Note how two very classy-sounding terms, *vista* and *focal point*, can change the entire way you look at your yard. You no longer are stuck with a backyard of lawn and shrubs. If you just pull out a sickly plant or two and add a sundial — Voilà! A vista in view! Now you have a place for your eyes to rest when they gaze out over the lawn, and perhaps the eyes of a critic won't notice that the lawn needs mowing or the weeds need pulling. A pleasant vista can help distract the mind from the details of reality. Just knowing your yard has a vista and a focal point makes it sound organized and well designed.

Exterior and Interior Vistas

The perfect garden vista is one that can be viewed from inside the house as well as outside in the garden. One great advantage of a vista easily seen from inside the house is that people no longer wonder when they catch you gazing off into space with that blank look on your face. Practice this statement: "Excuse me while I contemplate the vista." Now, you can daydream all you want and appear intelligent and well bred while you do it. Family members can be held at bay when there's a vista just outside the window. Practice snapping out this retort the next time your thoughts are interrupted by squabbling kids or a nagging spouse: "Don't talk to me now! My vista is in view!" Even single gardeners can take advantage of a vista they own. Want to get to know someone new? Invite him or her over to your house to view your garden vista. Just remember to open the drapes.

Exterior vistas are those best viewed from outside the garden. Anyone wishing to improve a house for resale should consider how the exterior vista or the curbside scene can be improved. The curbside appeal of your home is the way passersby and the neighbors across the street view the house from the curb. Real estate agents are hot about homes with curbside appeal, and many a great little vista has helped sell a house. By creating a little diversion with a path or arch in the front yard, you can lead the eyes of curbside lookers away from things such as dented garage doors and crooked gutters.

The quickest way to dress up a plain house is with an exterior vista. Even if you can't add dormer windows, a Palladian window, or hip roofs to your humble abode, you can make magic with a front yard courtyard, a cozy sitting spot, or a garden path and charming gate. All are landscaping tricks that grab and lead the eye.

Creating an interior vista to frame a view is usually enjoyed from inside the house as well as outside it. A great view is something to celebrate in any home or garden. If you have a waterfront lot, a mountain rising up in the distance, or just a pleasant city- or countryscape, frame it with plant material and direct the eye in the direction of the view.

A wide expanse of lawn with taller shrubs and a row of trees along the border is one way to frame a beautiful view if you have the 10 years it takes to wait for the trees and shrubs to mature. A shortcut is to use a fence line instead of a tree line and a flower border instead of a shrub border. And when you plan the shape of the beds, use an optical illusion to sound the trumpets on your great view. To do this, make the flowerbeds extra wide close to the house, then gradually narrow the width of the parallel beds as your property reaches out toward the view. Add even more eye trickery by concentrating cool blue and lavender flowers in the distance (these colors recede) and planning for warm, bright colors in the widest part of the beds near the house. This treatment gives more depth to the landscape. Now, your lovely view is colorfuly framed and formally presented.

In less formal gardens, a clearing through the native vegetation or a lowered section of fence line may be all that is necessary to frame a view. Country-style gardens look pleasing with an arch or arbor positioned so that the

TRELLISING: SCREEN OUT THE BAD
AND FOCUS ON THE GOOD

Trellising, or the art of growing plants on upright supports, is a quick shortcut to adding more height to the garden, screening out the undesirable, saving valuable ground space, and providing an attractive garden accent. A trellis can also be a focal point; examples are a latticework arch with roses for a country-style landscape or a tepee made with branches and covered with climbing nasturtiums for a naturalistic garden.

Any type of structure strong enough to support very fast-growing and enthusiastic vines can be used as a screen to frame views or as a pergola to lead the eye toward a view. Rustic trelliswork can be built from tree branches or unpainted cedar, and formal trelliswork can be purchased in wrought iron or built from brick and wood. You don't even have to put a vine on your trellis structure. Most vines need annual pruning to keep them in good control, but if you want a very formal and tidy look, plan on pruning your trellis garden at least three times a year.

Adding a trellis is a quick accenting shortcut.

view is channeled through the opening. One creative and literal-minded homeowner even built a large outdoor picture frame and positioned it on a rustic easel to perfectly frame his view of Mount Rainier.

Vistas to Organize a Cluttered Yard

Let's pare this organization idea down a bit and talk about how a vista can work in a mature or cluttered section of the yard, such as a perennial garden. (Perennials, as you may know, are those plants that return each year to bloom again and again. They include old-fashioned flowers such as irises, peonies, and daylilies.) Suppose you have a stunning perennial garden, but from a distance the whole thing looks like a mass of plant material with no pattern or reason. The vista shortcut can be put to use on this smaller scale by using stepping-stones through the plants to serve as a backbone. Now, even though the plants may be a jumbled mess, the stepping-stones give the eye a path to follow and the garden a sense of direction. Maintenance is also easier when a narrow pathway runs through a flower garden.

Another way to grab and lead the eye in a crowded garden is to use a dominant color or plant that acts as a frame or backbone for all the blooming extremities. For example, imagine a trail of silver dusty miller weaving through a flowerbed of predominantly pink and blue flowers. For that matter, any border of silver or gray foliage outlining a green lawn creates a visual path. The

QUICK-GROWING VINES TO COVER SCREENS, ARCHES, AND PERGOLAS

Honeysuckle: Sweet-smelling and demure, honeysuckle is perfect for a naturalistic or country-style garden.

Ivy: Predictable but dependable, ivy comes in so many forms and shades of green that it's worth searching different nurseries for just the right one. One worth hunting for is the large-leaved Algerian ivy and its variegated cousin. Both need more moisture than common English ivy, but the wider spacing between the leaves makes Algerian ivy seem a bit more formal. Plant ivy at the base of a cyclone fence and watch it grow into an evergreen hedge in about a year.

Kiwi: Hardy varieties and self-fertile varieties have made these imports very popular in the past couple of years. Don't expect much fruit unless you're faithful to pruning. They look great in contemporary gardens.

Wisteria: Graceful foliage and clusters of flowers that drip with understated elegance make this the quick-growing vine for formal and Oriental-style gardens.

contrast in color attracts the eye, and the repetition of this color leads it around. A contrast in shape or texture does the same thing.

One show garden I visited had a very unusual plant combination. A 4-foot-wide border of white, pink, and red petunias was accented with clumps of blue fescue, a wispy blue ornamental, grass. The blue grassy clumps were such a contrast to the soft-looking petals of the petunias that rather than adding more confusion to a flowerbed of many colors, the oddball ornamental grass grabbed the eye and led it toward the trellis of climbing roses in the background. This idea also works to add organization to a shrub border. Add plants of an unusual texture, such as the bamboolike *Nandina domestica*, and position them in a staggered line amid a shrub border. (*Nandina domestica* is sometimes called heavenly bamboo because it has the same graceful texture of bamboo but not its invasive root system.)

It's not important whether you use plants of a contrasting color and texture or stepping-stones in your crowded garden beds to create a vista, just as long as there is a contrast from the flower or shrub jungle and the pattern leads to a focal point at the end of the visual trail. Now, your crowded garden suddenly looks more organized and structured.

The point is that a vista can shape up your landscape no matter what shape it's in. The most important rule in creating a vista is to lead the eye toward a beautiful focal point and to screen or lead it away from the less attractive features of the house or landscape. Lead with a color, a path, a patch of lawn, rocks, or the repetition of certain plants. Put the two elements together — movement for the eye to follow and a resting spot at a focal point — and you've created a garden vista.

Vista Suggestions for Different Garden Styles

Plan your vistas now, and put them into practice as soon as you finish sprucing up the front entry. You don't even need to buy a lot of plant material to lay out your ideas for a great vista. There's no need to move hillsides and create valleys the way they did at the great estates. Remember, this is a book of shortcuts. Think small, and your results can still be as showy as the showcase gardens of your dreams. No matter how your vistas turn out, just having an excuse to contemplate vistas and look pensive instead of tuckered out at the end of the day is reason enough to start planning for a great garden vista now.

FORMAL/ESTATE VISTA

◆ A long narrow strip of lawn that ends at a fountain or statue is an example of a classic garden vista and focal point.

◆ On a smaller scale, consider a row of red geraniums that leads the eye to an urn overflowing with geraniums and ivy.

◆ A row of trees across a green lawn or a double row of trees and shrubs running alongside a driveway creates a neat and formal vista.

◆ A wide cement or brick pathway that ends with a formal front door makes a nice entry vista, especially if a low hedge of boxwood borders the walkway.

COUNTRY/COTTAGE VISTA

◆ Picture a garden path made of flagstone or brick that curves around a bed of flowers through a latticework arch bedecked with roses. The pathway leads your eye, and the rose-covered arch gives the path a place to go.

◆ A picket fence grabs and leads the eye, and a gate with a hanging basket of flowers on the post makes a charming focal point.

◆ Exposed aggregate cement or homemade stepping-stones work just about anywhere in a country-style garden — across the lawn or through the flowerbed. Just add a bench or other focal point at the end of the path.

◆ In the perennial flowerbed, use tall flowering plants such as hollyhocks, delphiniums, or sunflowers to grab the eye, and use a rose-covered trellis or arbor as the blooming focal point.

◆ For a scaled-down vista, arrange a gravel border along the edge of the bed and have it widen out a bit at the end to accommodate a stone frog, bunny, or other small feature.

CONTEMPORARY/ORIENTAL VISTA

◆ A gravel path or dry-rock streambed curving through a serene garden of low-growing evergreens is a calming vista in a Japanese-influenced garden. The placement of a stone pagoda or focal point tree in the background completes this soothing garden view.

- The use of large boulders leading to a bonsai or carefully pruned pine tree also leads the eye without cluttering the view.
- Use several berms or mounds of soil in a large yard to attract the eye toward a large focal point such as a contemporary work of art or a Japanese tea house. The berms could be planted with low-growing heather or Scotch moss.
- A series of posts with a length of thick chain creates a border and also leads the eye. Use a bridge over a gravel streambed as the focal point, and continue with the chain barrier as part of the railing on the bridge.
- Low-growing 'Hino' crimson azaleas are naturals for an Oriental-style garden, so make a trail of them leading toward a weeping cherry tree. You could substitute clumps of grassy irises for the azaleas in cold climates and use a star magnolia instead of a weeping cherry tree for the focal point.

NATURALISTIC/WOODLAND VISTA

- A natural-looking pathway of bark chips or a pine-needle carpet curving through a forest of vegetation can serve as a vista. If a rustic wooden bench is used at the end of the path, the seating will serve as a focal point. Whenever a path leads the eye to a bench or seating area, the look is soothing and relaxing.
- A riverbed of candelabra primroses grown in a low, wet spot can lead the eye toward a planted stump or moisture-loving calla lily.
- Ferns can be planted in colonies or large groups and arranged in graceful curves toward a small ornamental tree such as an Amur maple. You could substitute bleeding heart *(Dicentra)* for the ferns.
- Take advantage of a fallen log in a woodland garden and use it as a horizontal feature to lead the eye toward a taller focal point, such as a flowering dogwood or Japanese maple.

MEDITERRANEAN/DESERT VISTA

- Imagine a series of large boulders staggered out into the distance, leading the eye toward a giant cactus or pool of water. The surface between the boulders can be a gravel path or a sweep of sand.

- A row of clay pottery, either filled with bright gazania daisies or brightly painted and arranged in a line, draws one's attention toward a fountain or other courtyard feature.
- A clay tile pathway can be carried out beyond the porch area to extend toward the garden. Use a focal point, such a large cactus or a potted aloe plant, at the end of the path.
- A row of drought-tolerant acacia or eucalyptus trees can be used as a screen or to highlight a great view.

SUREFIRE SHORTCUTS

❖ If you use river rocks or gravel to create a dry streambed to lead the eye, spray shellac on the rocks to give them a shiny, wet look.

❖ If you want to lead the eye with a trail of formal-looking shrubs, space five or more compact-growing evergreen shrubs evenly apart in the direction of your focal point. Dwarf Alberta spruce are cone-shaped evergreens that can be used for this purpose.

❖ A quick way to lay a formal-looking pathway is to pile gravel on top of a sheet of cardboard or landscaping fabric and then lay stepping-stones in a contrasting color in the gravel. Position square stepping-stones on the diagonal so they resemble a diamond pattern.

❖ If you want a wider, more formal-looking path of stepping-stones, lay a double- or triple-wide row with gravel or grass packed in between the pavers.

❖ If you need to remove some overgrown shrubbery to create a clearing for a bench or container garden, don't worry about digging out the roots of the shrubs you cut down. Just saw off the trunks of such plants at ground level, cover them with a sheet of cardboard or landscape fabric, and layer a few inches of gravel on top. Now, add the bench or focal point on top of this gravel carpet.

❖ Sod busting is hard work. There is an easier way to kill the grass if you want to add a pathway or patio. Smother it with plastic, cardboard, or wooden boards. Without sunlight, a patch of lawn yellows and quickly dies, making it easier to remove.

Most-Asked Questions about Vistas

Q. *We want a formal look for our front yard, but we also want to eliminate a lot of lawn. What are our choices in inexpensive paving material besides the casual wood chip or gravel paths?*

A. Bricks are best for a formal look, and you can pave the surface for next to nothing if you're willing to scavenge for used bricks and lay them yourself on a sand base. Bargain bricks can be picked up at demolition sites (ask permission and be prepared to pay a small fee) and where new roads are being constructed over old brick roads. Contact the chimney sweeps in your area for leads on old brick chimneys that are being replaced. You can easily remove the mortar still attached to your used bricks by soaking them for a few hours in a wading pool and them chipping off the excess with a hammer and chisel. Check out a do-it-yourself book on brickwork for step-by-step instructions on laying brick. I know from personal experience that you don't need any special talent, just time and patience.

Q. *Our family room window looks out onto a steep bank that goes up a hillside. We would like to change this into a pleasant place to view and already own a recirculating fountain to work into the design. We need a low-maintenance solution to this steep problem and a way to draw attention to the fountain.*

A. Ground covers to the rescue! Steep banks need to be landscaped with thick plant material to prevent erosion and landslides. If your bank is sunny, ivy, hypericum, or juniper can survive. For a shady bank, use ajuga, vinca, or native ferns and wild violets. Next, to draw attention toward your focal point fountain, use a series of trails and steps to crisscross the bank and lead toward the fountain, or plant "rivers" of contrasting ground covers in sweeps up and down the hill, all meeting at the focal point. You need to trim the ground covers twice a year to keep them from growing into one another. Borders of timbers or rock also help to divide the different colors and textures on the hillside.

Q. *The view, or vista, from our patio is an ugly cinder block wall. Is there any magic trick that can turn this eyesore into a garden?*

A. Even without ground space, you can have a garden. The hard part is securing wood spacers to the masonry wall to act as holders for the half-baskets and brackets you need for vertical gardening. Hardware stores sell masonry screws for this use. You can make your own wall hangers using chicken wire and sphagnum moss. Bend the chicken wire around one half of a bowl to shape it and nail the sides and bottoms to the wall to form a pocket. Line it with moss, fill it with soil and plants, and care for it as you would a hanging moss basket.

Your wall garden will have a more formal look if you choose a focal point such as wall art and arrange the planters symmetrically on either side, with the larger baskets toward the center and smaller containers off to the sides.

Chapter Summary

❖ Adding a vista to a garden is a shortcut to a pleasant view.

❖ Creating a vista is as simple as leading the eye with the repetition of stepping-stones, a pathway, plants, or an expanse of lawn.

❖ Adding a pathway that leads to an arch, a bench, or some other focal point is an easy way to create a pleasant vista or view.

❖ Vistas can organize a cluttered or overgrown landscape by grabbing and leading the eye through the confusion.

CHAPTER 4

Focal Points, Features, and Accents: Shortcuts That Show Off Your Style

SHORTCUT:

Use nonliving focal points in your landscape for instant drama without added maintenance. Be creative and use any object that enhances your garden's style.

Let's get right to the goal of a garden focal point. Once you have created a view or vista in your yard, the focal point is what makes your landscape memorable. A focal point is any garden standout that anchors a scene, sets a mood, or catches the eye. The term *garden feature* usually refers to a birdbath, fountain, or some other outdoor object, whereas a focal point might be a feature, a sweeping view, a spectacular tree, or even the front door of the house. To complicate the garden lingo even further, garden features are sometimes called garden accents. Usually, the term *accent* refers to a feature that is smaller and less noticeable, perhaps a stone frog peeking from beneath a fern or a bit of trellis added to a fence.

You just have to realize that garden features, focal points, and accents are all fancy names for any outdoor garden doodad — from pink plastic flamingos to stone statues of Snow White and the Seven Dwarfs. Very upscale landscape designs may call for garden art in the landscape — a commissioned piece of abstract sculpture instead of a garden doodad, accent, or feature. What they all have in common is that they catch the eye and they're quick and easy enough for the impatient gardener to add to the landscape.

Focal points are often used in public and private show gardens. You may see focal points such as steel and stone sculptures on brass pedestals in contemporary parks or naked ladies draped in bed sheets in classic European gardens. Impressive displays of outdoor art do a lot to showcase public spaces and show gardens. There's no reason why you can't borrow this idea and use low-maintenance nonliving focal points to add interest and pizzazz to your own garden.

Experienced, green-thumbed gardeners may scoff at the idea of nonliving focal points gracing the garden. Horticultural wizards prefer to decorate the landscape with carefully pruned specimen plants, beautiful bonsai, or peaceful but demanding pools of water lilies. I offer a standing ovation to these talented and patient gardeners, but this chapter is not written for them.

Stone garden accents are quick, easy, and eye catching.

The focal points targeted here are of the instant gratification variety. Don't worry if you have a habit of killing the expensive plants that are supposed to make your garden breathtakingly beautiful. It's okay to admit that you resent all the effort and patience that goes into planting hundreds of tulips or nurturing a hedge of lilacs only to be rewarded with a few scant weeks of flowers. The focal points in this chapter are impossible to kill and look the same all year long. These are nonliving focal points that don't need weeding, feeding, or pleading to keep them at their eye-catching, scene-setting, mood-making best.

Focal Points and Features for Small Yards

You can forget about the statues of naked ladies draped with bed sheets if you garden on a typical city or suburban lot. Most homeowners find it in much better scale (and taste) to adorn their yards with more humble decorations befitting the style and size of the garden that they have.

It may help to remember that interior decorators add interest to a room with accent pieces such as baskets, vases, and framed photographs. The large elements of a room — the furniture, floor covers, and colors — are important, but it is the smaller touches that add flair and give a room that personal touch. Relate this to your outdoor rooms and you'll realize that the trees, shrubs, design, and layout are the large elements that form the landscape design. But to go from boring to beautiful, you need to dress up the space with smaller accents.

Now, don't curl your lip at garden features and accents if to you *cute* is a four-letter word. Small gardens needn't be playgrounds only for stone dwarfs and plastic bunnies. If country style touches and whimsical details distract you, there are focal points that add to the formal feeling or contemporary look you may want in your yard. Stick it out and keep reading to the end of this chapter. You'll find a list of focal points and features to enhance each of the five major garden styles.

For fun-loving gardeners who like to live on the whimsical side of the garden gate (the side with no design restrictions), don't be offended if the suggestions for garden

MORE FOCAL POINTS AND ACCENTS FOR SMALL GARDENS

❖ Wrought iron, wicker, or wooden chair instead of a bench

❖ Clay saucer filled with pebbles and seashells instead of a pond

❖ Painted pot holding a single geranium instead of a large mixed planter

❖ Garden plaque or decorative ceramic plant marker instead of a sundial

❖ Hanging birdbath that looks like a shallow dish, often sold with chain or wire hangers to suspend from a tree branch

❖ Half-baskets or wooden pots with one flat side for hanging from a nail in the wall instead of baskets or pots that hang from a roof overhang or extended bracket

❖ Small stone animals such as frogs, turtles, and birds on a life-size scale

features in this chapter don't include the whirligigs, plastic pets, or pink flamingos you find enchanting. The last chapter in this book is dedicated to the whimsy of extremely personal gardens that reflect the playful personalities of their owners. Even pink flamingos have their place.

I know of an upscale neighborhood where a couple left for the week to visit a tropical resort. "Don't bring back any tacky souvenirs," the neighbors said. "We've seen your bathroom towels, and we know how you love pink flamingos." The neighbors were kidding, of course, and going along with the joke, this couple promised to return with a suitcase full of plastic pink flamingos with wire legs to stick into the lawn. To their surprise, the neighbors beat them to the bird: On the couple's return from their trip, a flock of plastic pink flamingos was waiting to greet them, displayed prominently on the front lawn. Those flamingos became permanent focal points and are wonderful reminders of a great trip and a neighborhood with a sense of humor. If a garden focal point makes you and your neighbors smile and brings back pleasant memories, why not have them? In some landscapes, there really is a special place for plastic pink flamingos.

Stealing Focal Point Ideas from Show Gardens

If you haven't made a pilgrimage to a well-designed show garden, you're missing out on a lot of ideas for shortcuts. Although you can't duplicate the long avenues of flowering trees or billowing borders of perennials in your own backyard and call it a shortcut, there are hundreds of ideas free for the taking. Here in the Pacific Northwest, Minter Gardens and Butchart Gardens in British Columbia are two examples of show gardens that offer plenty of ideas for garden features and accents. There is a listing of show gardens to visit in Appendix A at the end of this book, and any gardener wishing to add spice or drama to the landscape need only invest in a walking tour of any of these fine gardens to be lured toward landscape improvement. Other ideas to inspire you can come from magazines, garden design books, neighbors, and the annual flower and garden shows that bloom in a few garden-crazy cities.

The trick to borrowing ideas from landscaping professionals is to cut through the glitter and glamour of these gorgeous gardens and focus on the style and look of the features and focal points. You may not be able to afford the hand-carved wooden bench that sets the scene at the display garden you love, but you can certainly echo that look with a simple park bench.

Garden art and focal points are big at the Northwest Flower and Garden Show, and every year the award-winning display gardens are accented with classy garden artworks: some are stone, others are contemporary wooden and

FLOWER AND GARDEN SHOWS

The four biggest flower and garden shows in the country are listed below. Telephone ahead for exact dates and locations, which may change from year to year.

Northwest Flower and Garden Show
Washington State Convention and Trade Center
1515 NW 51st Street
Seattle, WA 98107
(206) 789-5333

Philadelphia Flower Show
Philadelphia Civic Center
34th Street and Civic Center Boulevard
Philadelphia, PA 19104
(215) 625-8250

New York Flower Show
Pier 92, 51st Street and the Hudson River
New York, NY 10019
(212) 757-0915

New England Spring Flower Show
Bayside Exposition Center
200 Mount Vernon Street
Boston, MA 02125
(617) 536-9280

metal fixtures. One year, a country-style garden was awarded top honors by the judges. The outstanding display of blooming trees and shrubs grouped around a flagstone terrace at the top of a flight of wide stone steps was enough to make any gardener's green thumb itch. Sitting at the bottom of the stairway was an impressive pair of stone lions. Most of us don't live in homes grand enough to be guarded by a pair of lions, but don't dismiss the idea as one too overpowering to use at home. Just adapt the idea by positioning similar paired focal points at the bottom of your own front steps. Formalizing an entry with a matched set is an idea that can work anywhere.

The stone lions weren't the only impressive focal point in this award-winning garden scene. The carved stone bench at the top of the terrace added visually to the sense of welcome. Imagine the steps to your own front door or the path that leads to your porch and picture a pair of pots filled with flowering annuals acting as sentinels at the bottom of the steps or at the start of a path. Add a simple wooden bench (if there's room) on the porch next to the front door, and your home has acquired some of the same welcoming but formal feel that the impressive fantasy garden conveyed.

You can also adapt the stone lions by adding a stone pet to your garden. There has been a brisk business in stone frogs, cats, dogs, hedgehogs, and even pigs as garden decorations lately. Maybe it's because new materials make stonework more affordable, or perhaps gardeners have become tired of the damage done to the garden by real pets. Perfectly behaved dogs that never dig up flowerbeds are a gardener's dream.

Another advantage of visiting a flower and garden show or a show garden is that there are often vendors selling garden supplies, plants, and features. Large show gardens have a gift shop on the grounds. Either one may sell the perfect focal point for your garden style or the charming accent piece not found at the local hardware store or nursery. This is also where you can find the classic garden features used at show gardens and flower shows that adapt beautifully to smaller, more modest gardens. Another source of quality garden features is mail-order companies, whose array of birdbaths, sundials, and well-behaved stone pets may surprise you. (See Appendix.)

I must now utter a word of warning to homeowners visiting show gardens or garden shows for the first time. Try not to be overwhelmed by the use of color that fills these fantasy flower lands. Beds of blooming annuals and rows of roses are not the route to pursue if you want to take a shortcut to a showcase garden. Buying so many plants for mass color will break your budget, and tending all the flowers once they are planted will break your back. The best advice to viewers of such splendid gardens is to forget about the number of flowers used and focus on the focal points, the color schemes, and the layouts of the dreamscapes you encounter.

Color schemes are easy to imitate on a smaller scale in your own yard. When you visit a spectacular garden, take note of plants that bloom together beautifully, of pathway surfaces, and of colors of the garden focal points as they relate to the plants nearby. Write down what you like, then think of a way to scale down the idea so you can use it in your own yard.

A good example of how to change a show garden feature into a home

HOW TO ATTACK (INSTEAD OF JUST ATTEND) A FLOWER SHOW OR SHOW GARDEN

❖ Don't visit between the peak hours from noon to 4 p.m. Some shows offer a reduced price in the evening. By avoiding the crowds, you may have a chance to ask questions of the garden's designer or caretaker.

❖ Arm yourself with a notepad and a pen. You cannot possibly remember all the great ideas, color combinations, and plant names. Look at a scene, determine what catches your eye first, and write that down. This will help you figure out what appeals to you the most.

❖ Bring a camera, even if you hate to take photos. Pictures are the best way to record garden layouts and the quickest way to remember plant combinations.

❖ Bring a tote bag or backpack. Flower shows are bursting with vendors who offer free information and samples. You might also find just the right garden accent and need to lug it home.

❖ Be skeptical about unusual plants or blooming companions, especially at indoor garden shows. Often, the plants in the display gardens have been forced into bloom just for the show and are impossible to duplicate at home. Talk to the garden designers if you have questions about the natural blooming time of trees, shrubs, and flowers you admire. Always ask for the name of similar substitutes if the plants are marginally hardy in your area.

gardening shortcut is to imitate the waterfall and creek trickling through the show garden by using washed river rock and boulders in your landscape instead. The same blue-gray foliage from the irises that was so effective next to the pink primroses and boulders at the show garden can be used around your more practical dry creek bed. But only plant one clump of irises and six pink primroses instead of the two dozen iris clumps and hundreds of primroses you saw on display.

If you're still not inspired, or are simply in doubt about what kind of feature to add to your landscape, you can always lean on tradition. Choose from one of the classic garden features listed in the following section and you'll have plenty of award-winning garden designers who agree with your choice. Once you've chosen a garden accent or focal point, the next step is to showcase your investment by giving it proper placement in the garden.

Four Classic Garden Features

BIRDBATH

This is probably the most commonly used focal point in the typical American landscape, and yet, it is often not used to its best advantage. Birdbaths get tucked into the bushes and hidden from view, where they become dry and are forgotten. Even worse, hidden birdbaths can become lures for birds, which fall victim to marauding cats hiding in the overgrown shrubbery.

If you want to make a splash with a birdbath, dip into your pocketbook and invest in a heavy stone or cement version. (It took me 10 years and two tipped-over and broken birdbaths to reach the point where I recommend heavy-duty outdoor baths for birds.)

Sturdy and stylish are not the only things to consider if you want to use a birdbath to add drama, design, or birds to your landscape. It is the placement of the birdbath in your landscape that determines whether it adds to the beauty or blends in with the boring.

Good Places for a Birdbath

❖ ***In a clearing, away from tall shrubs and bushes.*** Overgrown shrubbery hides not only the garden feature you should show off but also bird-eating cats (that assume you purchased a birdbath just to lure birds out of the trees and into their clutches). For avian safety, overhead tree branches should be at least 15 feet away, and there should be no low-growing shrubbery thick enough to hide a cat.

❖ ***In the center of a flower garden.*** A colorful way to show off a birdbath and create an instant garden scene is to plant tall-growing flowers, such as snapdragons, in a semicircle behind the birdbath and low-growing ones, like petunias, in a semicircle in front. This circular frame of flowers shows off any garden feature. I'm still wondering about a déjà vu birdbath experience I had last summer. I was flipping through art prints at a variety store and stopped to admire a soft watercolor that showed a stone birdbath framed by pastel-colored snapdragons in the background with shorter yellow flowers growing in the foreground at the foot of the birdbath. It was one of those Impressionist-style paintings that have a blurry, dreamlike quality. Afterward, as I was driving home, I passed a front yard that looked just like the water color. (At this point, I

Plant tall-growing flowers in back and low-growing ones in front to frame any garden accent.

thought I heard the musical theme from "The Twilight Zone" playing in my head!) There could very well be a logical explanation for this coincidence. Perhaps the homeowners had the same art print I'd admired, or maybe a circle of flowers around a birdbath is just an art-inspiring design. Go ahead and duplicate this planting plan around your birdbath, and art lovers will do a double take as they drive past your home too.

❖ ***At a distance from people and activity in the yard.*** If you place a birdbath close to the front door, patio, or a kid's play area, it's likely to be knocked over, splashed in by kids, or used as a drop-off for mail and garden trowels. A birdbath placed close to people is inconsiderate of birds' modesty about bathing in public. The best spot for a birdbath, or any garden feature, is at the end of a vista, where it can be viewed from afar while sitting on the patio or gazing out the window. Serious bird-watchers consider a birdbath in plain view from a window essential.

❖ ***In the sun, if possible.*** Algae and mosquitoes breed in the moist, cool atmosphere of stagnant water.

❖ ***Ideally, close enough for the hose to reach or convenient enough to refill with a watering can.*** However, this is not important if you are using the birdbath for the way it looks in the garden and not to attract birds. Okay, I can hear squawks from bird lovers already. But, the truth is that many birdbaths displayed in fine gardens are more decorative than avian attracting, and the focus of this book is not on attracting birds but on making the garden more attractive. Birds do, however, add beauty, eat insects, and fill the air with song. See the box on page 77 titled "The Bird Lover's Birdbath" if adding a birdbath means more to you than just having a great-looking focal point. There also are many wonderful books written about how to attract birds to the garden, and they include specifications for the perfect depth and location of birdbaths. If the birds become cleaner and hang out in your yard as a by-product of the landscaping process, you win in two ways.

Plants to Use around a Birdbath

A birdbath that is actually used will create swamplike conditions in its vicinity. When birds bathe, they really splash. Plants that like this extra moisture but that won't serve as cat camouflage are impatiens, pansies, ajuga, bugleweed, and a delightful-smelling, very low ground cover called Corsican mint.

In formal or desert gardens, a 2-foot-wide border of gravel or bricks around the birdfeeder or the birdbath might be preferred instead of plants. Remove at least 3 inches of soil before filling the border with gravel. This will prevent spilled birdseed from becoming wild bird weeds, and soil from becoming mud.

BENCH

There are probably more photographs, paintings, and daydreams of benches placed perfectly in the garden than of any other feature. You can buy or easily build a bench to enhance any garden style, from Victorian to contemporary. If I were to recommend one garden feature to personalize a mundane landscape, it would be some type of outdoor seating.

When deciding what type of outdoor seating to invest in, be honest about how much actual sitting will take place. If you just want a stately focal point at the end of a brick path, a no-maintenance classic stone bench is ideal. But, if you've ever tried to sit on a stone bench and read the paper or open the mail, you already know what my complaint is. Stone and cement seating is hard on the body.

THE BIRD LOVER'S BIRDBATH

It's easy to make a functional birdbath. In nature, birds use any spot that collects water to drink and bathe. A shallow dish set on a stump or flat stone will bring birds to your garden if you remember to provide clean water. It's not important to the birds how the bath looks; it's more important that you observe these rules:

❖ Larger is better. Some birds like to bathe in flocks, so a bath at least 2 feet wide allows more than one bather at a time. If the birdbath is smaller than 1 foot across, the birds will drink from it but not bathe in it.

❖ Don't have a slippery bottom. A textured surface is best, but if you need to add a nonslip surface, add gravel, sand, or bathtub decals.

❖ Don't make the water too deep. Most birds won't go in water deeper than 2 to 3 inches. Add stones to the deepest part of your birdbath to make the birds more secure.

❖ Birds don't like black bottoms. They can't tell how deep the water is unless the bottom is light in color.

❖ Keep any vegetation near the birdbath too low and sparse to hide a cat. An overhanging branch from a nearby tree makes an ideal security roost for the birds (not the cat).

The most comfortable outdoor seating is the wood-frame style with removable (and comfortable) cushions. The problem is that the cushions don't weather well, and one sudden rainstorm can melt all of the comfort away. Unless you have a covered patio or porch, it's best to use outdoor seating that can stay outdoors, at least during the summer months.

A compromise among good looks, low maintenance, and comfort is the iron-and-wood park-style bench. We've had one on our brick courtyard for almost 10 years. It sits out all winter, and the wood slats have finally lost their stained protection and are now supporting a colony of lichen and a bit of moss. I should probably clean the wood and restain the surface, but the slightly woodsy look of those worn-out slats seems to match the moss-covered, well-worn patina of our used brick courtyard. Even if your outdoor bench is never really used, just viewing a seat in the landscape gives a feeling of instant relaxation.

Good Places for a Bench

❖ At the end of a path, to offer respite and reward to garden wanderers

❖ On the front porch, to make the main entry appear welcoming and inviting (Remember the earlier story of the winning show garden?)

❖ In the center of a courtyard, to change it from a place that is walked through to a place that is cherished as a retreat

❖ Tucked into a niche carved out of the shrubs or alongside a wide spot in a garden path

❖ Back in the woods or around a bend or bush as a feature to discover in a secret garden

❖ Under an arbor or an outdoor arch

❖ The spot where you most need seating — near the mailbox, where kids wait for the school bus, or in a sunny corner you'd like to enjoy (actually using your outdoor seating is even nicer than just viewing it)

Plants to Use around a Bench

❖ Low-growing, fragrant plants work best to entice you to enjoy the bench. If you place a bench in a sunny spot, many of the easy-care, sun-loving herbs such as lavender, santolina, and thyme ease in comfortably and fragrantly beside it. Consider contrasting these gray-foliaged, fragrant herbs with pink-blooming dianthus or blue lobelia.

❖ Use taller, fragrant shrubs for the background plantings near your bench. Lilacs, mock orange, choisya, butterfly bush, and daphne are just some of the possible blooming shrubs that engulf the weary gardener in fragrance if planted behind a resting spot. And

Plant a fragrance garden around your bench.

don't forget the roses. A rose arbor behind a bench, a hedge of roses beside a bench, or potted rose trees on either side of a bench can turn even the most humble seating into a floral fantasy of sight and smell.

❖ For a more formal garden, a large pot on either side of a garden bench frames the bench and adds to the formal feeling. Stiff, upright plants such as geraniums, rose trees, boxwoods, or dwarf evergreens are the plants traditionally used in these pots.

❖ Roses growing on an arbor, lilacs forming a niche in a hedge, or ferns framing a clearing in the woods can also add to the look you wish to achieve around the bench.

A Three-Step Plan for Creating Beautiful Bench Marks

Step 1: Choose the location and invest in the bench that best suits your garden style.

Step 2: Lay a foundation of bricks, bark, gravel, or flagstones under the seating area. Choose the surface that best complements the style of your bench and area.

Step 3: Add pots on either side of the bench and, plant a hedge or background plants to frame the scene.

SUNDIAL

Brightening your landscape with a sundial does more than just keep track of the sunny hours in your garden. Place a sundial on a simple pedestal and group a collection of roses or herbs around it for an instant theme garden. Sundials have been gracing courtyards since ancient times, when they had a mystical appeal because only wizards could figure out how to construct them properly. During the Middle Ages, advancements in math made sundials easy enough for craftsmen to construct and made the sundial a more affordable and common garden feature. The sun began to set on sundial popularity in the 1920s, but in the past 10 years, there has been dawning interest in this traditional garden feature.

Good Places for a Sundial

❖   In the middle of a brick or gravel courtyard

❖   At the end of a path or vista

❖   In rose, herb, perennial, or fragrant gardens, or in any special garden

❖   Beneath an upstairs window so it can be viewed from above

❖   Ideally, but not necessarily, in full sun; you're using this feature as a shortcut, not as a timepiece.

Plants to Use around a Sundial

I can't resist suggesting creeping thyme, lemon thyme, and mother-of-thyme as perfect sundial companions. Then you will enjoy thyme on your hands whenever you work near the sundial.

Changing a Sundial to Suit Your Style

A sundial fits best into a formal or traditional landscape, but by using some creativity, you can create a sundial scene for a contemporary, woodland, or desert garden.

❖   In a contemporary/Oriental landscape: Display on a cube or rectangular pedestal made of wood or cement. Improvise by using a cement culvert pipe stood on end as a pedestal. The smooth sides and simple lines of the cement pipe look very contemporary.

Most culvert pipes have a flared end that adds to the pedestal look. If your sundial is too small to balance on top of the pipe, mount a round cement stepping-stone on the end of the pipe, then add the sundial. Sundials can also be made from polished stone or steel. They don't have to be in traditional brass with Roman numerals and script.

❖ In a woodland garden: Picture a sundial perched on a large boulder with ferns at its base. You can also use an old stump or low fence post as a more casual pedestal in a garden of native plants. You can help a sundial adhere to an unusual surface by using sticky florist's clay.

Try planting herbs at the base of a sundial.

The Great Sundial Hunt

Finding an affordable sundial used to be a hopeless task. The large brass works of art offered in fine garden magazines were usually imported from Europe and terribly expensive. All that has changed. I have seen sundials for sale at garden centers, nurseries, and hardware stores; some drugstores even carry them in their gift departments. There also are tiny indoor sundials to set on the windowsill near houseplants that can become a feature for indoor gardens.

Finding a pedestal for your sundial is a little more difficult. Except for improvising with fence posts, stumps, and culvert pipes, the best idea for a sundial base is a birdbath base. I found this out the hard way.

If you read the previous section on birdbaths, you'll remember that I warned of the dangers of setting a birdbath near a source of activity. I spoke from experience. The terra-cotta birdbath in our rose garden was tipped over by a curious child (one of mine) and the bathing basin shattered. It took a while, but I finally figured out what to do with the topless birdbath pedestal. A sundial would not rest on the top because the pedestal tapered to a narrow width at the

PLANTING IN RECYCLED CONTAINERS

Recycling odd pieces of junk as plant containers is more than just a low-budget way to pot up plants: Rescue anything that might end up occupying space in a landfill and become an environmental hero. Look for creative containers at the dump, tag and garage sales, and surplus stores. Here are some guidelines for recycling containers and turning your trash into treasures:

❖ Don't actually plant in the container. Use a plastic pot to slip inside the opening instead. Its easy to rotate blooming plants by lifting out the pot of faded blooms and slipping in another fresh pot of the same size.

❖ Pillow plantings are the answer to odd-shaped containers. Just use a plastic bag of potting soil, and tie up the ends so that none of the soil can escape. Freezer bags work well and come in many sizes. Make slits in the bottom for drainage and slits in the top to add the plants. The plastic bag of soil conforms to the shape of any pot. You can also skip using a pot and set the plastic "pillow" of soil on a table (with a protective liner underneath) as a centerpiece. Draping plants such as petunias and ivy will soon cover the plastic casing.

❖ A can of enamel spray paint quickly freshens up well-worn surfaces.

top. Only when I turned the birdbath base upside down did I realize that the flared bottom was wide enough for a sundial. I placed the narrow end in a large clay pot of soil and drove a wooden stake down through the base's hollow top for stability. Now the wider end that was sticking up (which used to be the base of the birdbath) flared out for a 12-inch sundial to rest on. The result was a sun-loving, tiered terra-cotta planter with a sundial in the middle. The whole thing sits in the middle of my brick courtyard and looks perfectly at home.

CONTAINER

Plants growing in pots have always been the quickest way to dress up any home landscape. This includes everything from clay pots of petunias to cement

- ❖ Turn a group of unrelated small containers into a collection by painting them all the same color. Arrange them in groups of three to five with matching plants to coordinate the group further.

- ❖ Show off a collection of related objects by grouping them. Nail series of recycled tin canisters to a wooden fence and plant them with herbs, or create a display of "saved soles" — old leather boots and shoes lining the steps or sitting on top of a wall and planted with hen and chickens and burro's tail.

- ❖ Hanging plants can be grown in almost anything with a handle. Suspend a leaky bucket by its handle on a wall bracket or fence post. Let an ivy geranium or lotus vine spill over the sides.

- ❖ Baskets can always be recycled. Line them with heavy plastic garbage bags or a pillow pack, or find the perfect size of plastic pot to drop into the basket.

urns with ivy or bonsai. To make effective use of these potted focal points, give them a great location. Container gardens look right at home when nestled next to a bench or in the center of a theme garden, and large pots can even by used as focal points on a lawn or in a flowerbed. Just spread a gravel base or lay a stepping-stone down first for the container to sit on.

Container gardens often do double duty as focal points and as solutions for all sorts of gardening problems. Pot up the problem — from poor soil to slug invasions. A few large pots can also change the behavior of misbehaving pets.

I remember a family who, in one step, trained their dogs, cleaned up the porch, and put color close to the front door. Their landscape was a casual country style, and the mood was set by a low-roofed rambler and a western-style post-and-board fence framing the yard. The wide overhang of the roof meant that the entry garden next to the front door was dry, shady, and cool in summer, a fact that the two large Labrador retrievers that owned the family took advantage of. These dogs took to napping in the entryway flowerbeds and digging hollows in the dirt to lie in. As a result, the cement pad that served as an entry always needed sweeping. The owners tried planting all sorts of hardy evergreen plants that might stand up to the digging dogs, but nothing survived. Finally, they shoveled gravel over the dusty dirt and set two large tubs of shade-loving impatiens on top of the gravel bed. When I say tubs, I mean shiny aluminum ones, the size of a washtub. This novel idea could be rewritten using any style container.

After only a few hours of nosing around the heavy pots, the dogs started checking out the yard for a new napping spot. Now, when visitors ring the front bell, they have an interesting and blooming focal point to gaze on while waiting for the door to open. Whenever an unusual focal piece is used near the front door, it works wonderfully to distract your guests from an unweeded flowerbed or an unmown lawn.

Create a focal point with a container filled with annual flowers.

In case you're wondering about the two lazy dogs, they learned to adjust. The last time I pulled into the driveway at this home, the two didn't bother to move from their new napping spot in the shade of a tree that overhangs the gravel drive. They just wagged their tails at the horn honking and continued to block the drive so that I was forced to abandon my automobile in disgust and walk around the happy pair. Only then did these friendly watchdogs awaken and amble over for a tail-wagging greeting.

Other examples of unusual objects that can become containers in casual gardens are milk cans, wooden barrels, wooden carts, wagons, and even old baby buggies. Just about anything you love and that can take the weather can be used as an outdoor container. Remember, you don't need to plant directly in the decorative container: Use it instead as a sleeve for a smaller pot with drainage holes.

One of my younger brothers made good use of a metal artillery shell casing by turning it into a pedestal pot for an ivy plant. The shell stands 3 feet tall with the tip removed (blown off, he says) and the hollow inside exposed. It was simple enough to find a plastic pot with a rim of the perfect size to nestle inside the casing. Most of the pot is hidden as it sinks into the bullet-shaped shell, and the outer rim of the pot keeps it from slipping all the way down. A rocket-shaped plant stand goes quite well with the rest of this bachelor's interior nondesign. It would be a really explosive success if only the poor ivy plant wasn't dead and brown. On second thought, he probably thinks a dead plant fits with the theme of the army surplus container.

If you need more encouragement to break away from the traditional family of garden accents, study Chapter 7, The Finishing Touch, on garden whimsy and personal style.

Just Your Style: Garden Features That Enhance Specific Styles

FORMAL/ESTATE STYLE

- Cement or terra-cotta urns
- Bronze sundials
- Stone cherubs
- Cement birdbaths
- Wrought-iron or stone benches
- Busts or sculptures displayed on columns or pedestals
- Flagpoles ringed with flowers the same color as the flag
- Pools with fountains or water lilies
- Wall-mounted fountains
- Decorative iron gates

COUNTRY/COTTAGE STYLE

- Decorative birdhouses or dovecotes
- Bronze sundials
- Stone animals
- Decorative watering cans sitting on the porch or atop a garden wall
- Stone birdbaths
- Baskets filled with ivy or flowers
- Hanging moss baskets
- Wooden benches with backs or park-style benches

CONTEMPORARY/ORIENTAL STYLE

- Large boulders used in groups, with gravel or sand around the bases
- Metal sculptures of cranes
- Stone pagodas and towers
- Small pools or carved rocks filled with water
- Stone frogs or turtles in life-sized scale
- Groupings of polished rocks or flat stones sprayed with shellac to make them shiny
- Areas of sand raked into patterns
- Bonsai in containers or trees pruned into bonsai shapes
- Simple cement slab benches

NATURALISTIC/WOODLAND STYLE

- Rustic birdhouses
- Birdbaths of curved stones or recycled material
- Stone woodland animals
- Hollowed-out tree stumps filled with flowers
- Logs carved in the shapes of bears or other woodland creatures
- Unpainted, rustic benches or twig tables and chairs
- Bird feeders
- Recycled wheelbarrows or other material showing signs of age and used as planters
- Whiskey-barrel ponds or water gardens

Fill a hollowed-out stump with flowers.

MEDITERRANEAN/DESERT STYLE

- Wagon wheels
- Steer skulls nailed to the fence or displayed on a gravel floor
- Large boulders with sedums and succulents planted at their bases
- Farm tools displayed on the side of the building
- Seating made from wooden barrels

- Cowboy boots displayed on the front porch or planted with sedums
- Driftwood or bleached wood displayed with sand and gravel
- Tiled fountains

SUREFIRE SHORTCUTS

❖ Two pots at the beginning of a path act as focal points to formalize any entry.

❖ Mail-order catalogs can be a source of high-quality garden focal points and save you time, too.

❖ Pedestals — a stump, pipe, or overturned pot — can help display your garden art. Stone animals, sundials, birdhouses, and contemporary sculptures carry more weight in your landscape when placed on a pedestal.

❖ Giant pots are good for containers, but don't plant in them. Fill them half-way with gravel or Styrofoam pellets, then set plastic pots filled with flowers into the larger, dressy containers, which allows you to keep color constantly in your show pots by replacing the plastic pots with blooms of seasonal color.

❖ An old wooden wheelbarrow makes a great container garden. Set pots of flowers in the wheelbarrow and cover the tops of these containers with bark dust, moss, or a similar mulch to create a portable color spot.

❖ Leaky metal watering cans can be dressed up with spray paint and set near the porch or a pathway as a garden ornament.

❖ A tall focal point is easy to create: mount a birdhouse or wind sock on top of a wooden dowel or steel pipe.

❖ Turn a stump or wooden post into a focal point by nailing a flock of birdhouses to the sides. Use whimsical, traditional, or country-style birdhouses, depending on your garden style.

Most-Asked Questions about
Focal Points, Features, and Accents

Q. *We moved into an older home, and the front yard is dominated by one large cherry tree. This tree is gorgeous in spring but is still the focus of the yard after it blooms. Is there anything we can do to draw attention away from it? We're tempted to cry, "Timber!"*

A. Remain calm and do not make any rash decisions. It takes years to grow a large tree but only minutes to chop it down. If the cherry is healthy and gorgeous every spring, why not play up the pink blossoms by adding drifts of pink tulips to the landscape? Choose a tulip variety that blooms at the same time as the cherry tree. Once summer arrives, you can still have color by using the tree branches as hooks for hanging baskets. Make sure the limbs are strong enough, them hang them with baskets of shade-loving fuchsias and impatiens. (These same flowers will also bloom in the shade in pots beneath the tree.) It will be easier to grow annuals in containers than to try to plant in the root-infested ground at the base of the mature tree. In autumn, add color and accent with a pumpkin display, cornstalk bundles, or a scarecrow propped against the trunk. In winter, decorate the branches with tiny white lights. Big, old trees can remain attractive, four-season focal points if you change your landscaping with the season.

Q. *I'm the type of person who accidentally kills plants and would like to have a no-maintenace yard. I already have quite a collection of stone animals and outdoor garden accents because even I can't damage them. I would like to tear out all the lawn, replace it with gravel, and add to my collection of garden ornaments rather than having plants. My husband claims this would not look good. What is your opinion?*

A. Sorry to disappoint you, but all accents and no plants is no garden at all. Your charming little stone animals would cease to be accents or focal points because they would no longer catch the eye, but instead, would clutter the property. A good rule is to have only one accent in view at any one point.

It sounds as though what you really need is basic gardening information and help in finding the right plants for your yard. When the right plants are placed in the proper locations, very little routine maintenance is required — and then I promise even you can have a yard that looks like a garden, not an accent sales lot. Landscape designers, nursery people, and other horticultural professionals can recommend plants and study materials for low-maintenance gardening in your area.

Q. *Can benches and fountains be left out all winter? How about the expensive pots I purchased?*

A. If it freezes, you could get burned. Clay and terra-cotta pottery can crack and break during freezing and thawing, and recirculating fountains can freeze up and burn out the motor. Iron furniture can rust, wood can warp, and paint can peel. The most conscientious gardeners winter their outdoor accents in a garage or covered area. Keeping moisture away from clay pottery when the weather is freezing reduces the chance of its cracking, but in areas with severe winters, wooden containers are recommended. Items too heavy to move can be protected during severe cold snaps with tarps. Outdoor furniture only needs to be moved to a covered porch or patio.

Routine maintenance of these items includes periodically staining or oiling wooden furniture and planting pots, using a rust-inhibiting spray paint on iron furniture, and cleaning the accumulated salt and algae off clay pots with a brush and a solution of bleach and water.

Chapter Summary

❖ Add nonliving focal points or garden features that catch the eye to quickly dress up a landscape.

❖ Visit show gardens or flower and garden shows to find ideas and to purchase garden focal points.

❖ Choose a garden feature that complements the style of your landscape, or choose from one of the classics: a birdbath, sundial, bench, or container.

❖ Display your garden feature at the end of a vista and enhance it with companion plantings or open space.

CHAPTER 5

Showcase Your Show-Off Plants

SHORTCUT:

Accentuate the best-looking plants in your landscape. Show-case, spotlight, and show off what you grow best.

Beautiful plants are the backbone of any spectacular landscape. You can accent all you want with pathways, vistas and great-looking outdoor art, but a garden isn't a garden without plants. These are the shortcuts you can take to highlight the best-looking plants in your yard, even if you haven't either a green thumb or the time to fuss over anything exotic.

I'm not going to tell you about gardening tips for better plant care. I've already written that book. (In *Tips for Carefree Landscapes,* I ramble on about the easiest-to-grow plants and how to care for them.) This chapter includes suggestions for carefree, show-off plants, but more important, it teaches you how to draw attention to the beautiful plants you already have — wonderful specimens that aren't drawing the compliments and attention they deserve.

This chapter also is for those of you who may already have trophy plants such as a fantastic flowering tree or a gorgeous Japanese maple and want to show it off. The art of accentuation is like turning up the volume on the lyrical beauty of your favorite plants. These are the shortcuts that make the colors of your flowers shout instead of whisper. These simple tips make the beautiful shape of your specimen trees stand out instead of sit down, and the gracefulness of your hanging baskets shine like a beacon instead of blending into boredom. This collection of show-off shortcuts spotlights everything that is good in your garden.

FOUR SEASONAL PERFORMERS AND THEIR SHOWY SIDEKICKS

Forsythia (*Forsythia* species)

About the only attributes of this casually sprawling shrub is the bright yellow blooms that cover the plant in early spring and its nondemanding attitude. Grow forsythia in a sunny spot away from the house or you'll need to do annual pruning to keep it under control. In cold winter areas, give it protection from the wind, or the buds may freeze before they bloom. Prune immediately after blooming or just before the buds burst if you want to bring the branches indoors to force into flower.

Blooming sidekicks: Early bulbs such as crocus, grape hyacinth, and snowdrop planted at the foot of forsythia help draw attention to the shrub during its early-spring glory days. The blossoms of these early-blooming bulbs fade about the same time as the forsythia blooms end, and the entire scene can fade into the background.

Beauty Bush *(Kolkwitzia amabilis)*

Old-fashioned, hard to kill, and a dependable bloomer when given a sunny spot, this shrub is definitely easy to ignore except for the short amount of time it is covered with pink blossoms in late May. Use beauty bush in the back of the garden border because it can grow over 10 feet tall and almost as wide. Prune to shape, but only after it has bloomed.

Blooming sidekicks: Bearded irises, white candytufts, late-blooming Darwin tulips, sea thrift, and poppies are just a few of the May-blooming perennials that bloom in tandem with beauty bush.

Old-Fashioned Weigela *(Weigela florida)*

When not in bloom, this adaptable shrub is coarse and rangy, but for a week or two in late spring, nothing could be finer than the arching branches covered with white, red, or pink bell-shaped blossoms. In very cold climates, look for the variety 'Venusta', which has been bred so the blossoms won't freeze. Prune this shrub after it blooms to control its enthusiasm and tidy its form.

Blooming sidekicks: Weigela blooms a little later than beauty bush, but the same perennials can be used to draw attention to its blossoms. Easy-to-grow perennials that bloom at approximately the same time are irises, late tulip, white candytuft, and pink sea thrift.

Rose of Sharon *(Hibiscus syriacus)*

This stiff, upright shrub is downright ugly most of the year because it is one of the last things to sprout leaves in spring and the first to drop them in fall. Its frequent nakedness is quickly forgiven, however, as soon as the large, tropical-looking blooms appear. Rose of Sharon blooms in late summer when the rest of the garden is getting tired and seedy. The fine, fat buds open to white, blue, or purple blossoms, and most varieties sport an attractive darker eye in the center. Grow in sun or partial shade and well-drained but not dry soil, and give it room. This shrub can be pruned into a tree shape if space is limited.

Blooming sidekicks: Purple and pink asters not only have the deep colors that look great with hibiscus, but they share the same bloom time as well. The autumn-blooming crocus and early-blooming garden mum are other companions that look their best in late summer and early fall, just as Rosie gets ready to put on a show.

How to Decide Which Plants Have Star Quality

There are different ways to audition your plants and determine which ones deserve the spotlight. You could choose the seasonal performers. These plain members of the garden dress up but once a year to become blossom-covered princesses. But, like Cinderella, the regal finery is short-lived and when the flowers have faded, these plants once again wear the inconspicuous garden green uniform of a commoner. Seasonal performers are shrubs such as forsythia, weigela, beauty bush, and rose of Sharon or hibiscus. All four have short, vibrant displays of color that can't be missed, followed by lackluster foliage that blends into the background the rest of the year. Seasonal performers need to be highlighted only for a few weeks when they are in bloom. Adding some low-growing companions that bloom at the same time draws attention to the short but showy performance of these seasonal beauties. Position these shrubs near the back of a flowerbed or as a bush border along

FOUR TREES THAT LOOK GREAT 4 SEASONS OF THE YEAR

Japanese Maple *(Acer palmatum)*

Delicate and deeply lobed leaves and a small but refined stature make this a lovely year-round specimen for any style of garden, although Japanese and contemporary landscapes use this plant most often. There are Japanese maples with varying shades of red or green leaves and grafted specimens that stay low and compact. Grow these well-behaved maples on a mound, surrounded by a few boulders, or use them as living artwork, displaying their attractive branches against the blank canvas of a bare expanse of wall.

Flowering Dogwood *(Cornus florida)*

Although the Korean dogwood *(Cornus kousa)* is more disease resistant, both types have good winter form, fall color, and attractive blossoms. Woodland gardens and country-style landscapes seem to cry out for this cheerful little tree, but dogwoods are also used in traditional Japanese gardens.

Flowering Crab Apple *(Malus floribunda)*

Red-to-pink blossoms decorate the branches in spring, followed by richly colored summer foliage and red or yellow fruit in the fall. The growth habit of this street tree favorite is tidy and compact, so it requires little pruning, even in small gardens. Some varieties, such as 'Hopa', are fragrant as well as beautiful, but disease problems make this variety difficult to grow anywhere except the hot-summer areas found in southern California. There are so many crab apples to choose from that it pays to talk to a local nursery manager and get a specific recommendation for your area. Any style of garden would be enhanced by a crab apple.

Weeping Atlas Cedar (*Cedrus atlantica* 'Pendula')

A slow-growing evergreen with blue-gray needles and vertically drooping branches, this specimen tree can be trained into an arch or unusually twisted shape. This is definitely a plant that catches the eye all year long, but it requires more care and knowledgeable pruning than most specimen trees. The blue color makes it stand out handsomely when surrounded by a green lawn. Formal, Japanese, and naturalistic gardens are the styles most likely to display this majestic weeper as a focal point plant.

the property line. They are all large enough to be enjoyed from a distance and don't really deserve a place of honor up close to the house or near a pathway. Be sure you don't block the view of their beauty with taller plants during the short time they are in full bloom.

There also are some very valuable plants that display good form and color all year long. These are usually trees and shrubs with color in fall and spring and attractive bark and branch patterns in summer and winter. Many evergreen and needle-leaved plants also have this year-long season of beauty, although it is the form and shape of the plant and not the changing leaf color or blossoms that make it an interesting specimen. Most of the tips for showcasing spectacular plants are meant for the long-running players that look great most of the year.

There are other reasons to highlight a particular plant besides the fact that it is a seasonal bloomer or has interesting features for four seasons of the year. You may want to show off a favorite rose plant that blooms repeatedly all summer long or wish to highlight a climbing vine that drapes gracefully over an archway. Some gardeners are proud of their bedding plants and want full attention paid to their carpets of color, whereas others prefer the subtle beauty of texture and form that herbs lend to a planting bed. Specialty growers of dahlias, daylilies, or daffodils may want to highlight their collection during the peak period of bloom, while other homeowners want only to distract the eye from a sparse-looking lawn or ugly view and highlight the plants that are healthy and growing in the yard.

How to Set Off Specimen Plants

You can choose to honor any plant or area in your landscape for any reason at all by using the tips in this section to frame your favorites and highlight the positive.

FRAME IT WITH SPACE

If you want to dress up your yard in a hurry, consider removing rather than adding plants. Yes, you read that right: Subtracting plants can be an addition to your landscape.

If you have a mature garden, you probably have at least one lovely specimen on your property already, but chances are it's buried in a jungle of shrubbery. Clear out the overgrown and overplanted underlings from beneath that gorgeous tree or beautiful shrub and let the empty space become a frame to show off the good looks of your favorite plant.

When your healthy trees and shrubs begin to grow too big for their beds, don't automatically punish them with the pruning shears. Remember, you're the one who's been fertilizing and watering to encourage all the new growth you now want to amputate. Consider instead removing some of the lawn to make a bigger planting bed or thinning out less desirable plants to create more space around the plant that really looks good. Successful plant growers are often the ones most guilty of overplanting their gardens. The plants keep getting bigger and bigger, and the space between them grows smaller and smaller. Soon, the landscape is nothing more than a jungle of growth that lacks the beauty of empty space and the individual character of single plants. Many plants look best when displayed in groups (flowering bulbs and birch trees come to mind), but unusual trees and shrubs shine brighter without the distracting competition of nearby neighbors.

I remember the year our town suffered through an unusually hard winter. The icy winds froze out an entire hedge of low-growing hebe from around a contorted filbert in our front yard. (I should take a moment to explain that a contorted filbert grows more like a shrub than a tree and has many twisted and contorted branches breaking from ground level and spiraling upward like gnarled fingers. It is definitely an unusual specimen that is best appreciated in the winter months when a lack of foliage allows the corkscrew pattern of the branches to be seen. Hebe is a dense evergreen shrub, and the variety I had been growing looked similar in appearance to boxwood. The plants had been growing in a semicircle around the filbert tree until the winter storm turned them into works of ice.)

The loss of a dozen choice plants is hard for any gardener, and I was prepared for my gardening friends and family to gasp in horror at the missing hebe hedge and the emptiness around the filbert tree. Time passed, and I never heard a murmur of sympathy. Instead, I began to realize that the loss had actually improved the look of the contorted filbert tree, especially when even my husband commented on the improvement. Joe is not the kind of guy who notices plants and flowers, so it was unusual when he looked outside and said, "Hey, when did you get that neat-looking tree?" That neat-looking tree had been growing right outside the window for the past 5 years. It had just blended quietly into the shrubbery jungle until the hebe plants had defoliated and the hedge disappeared, revealing our treasure tree.

UNUSUAL SPECIMEN PLANTS

Topiary Artwork

Topiary is the art of pruning compact evergreens such as yew or boxwood into unusual shapes. Animals and geometric shapes are the most common, but shrubs pruned to look like giant baskets or pieces of furniture are also examples of topiary.

Wire forms are sometimes made into the shapes of animals or objects, and ivy or other vines are trained to cover the forms. Topiary shapes can be grown a lot sooner with this method than by waiting for shrubs to grow to size.

Peegee Hydrangea Tree (*Hydrangea paniculata* 'Grandiflora')

This shrub-tree sports such huge heads of blooms in late summer that anything blooming nearby is dwarfed. This arresting specimen looks best surrounded by lawn or ground cover.

Weeping Siberian Pea Tree (*Caragana arborescens* 'Pendula') and Weeping Pussy Willow (*Salix discolor* 'Pendula')

Both of these small trees have weeping branches grafted to a central trunk, giving them a very unusual and exotic look. They are more the size of a small shrub than a tree, so growing them on a mound adds impact to their unusual shape.

Standard or Tree Forms of Grafted Evergreens

Pines, cotoneaster, and members of the cedar family are sometimes grafted and sold as novelties or specimen plants at nurseries. Display these small "trees" with lots of space around them to show off their formal tree form.

Twisted Corkscrew Willow (*Salix matsudana* 'Tortuosa')

The last part of its scientific name says it all. The branches of this willow look like they have been tortured, and the twisted appearance is very similar to that of the contorted filbert (*Corylus avellana* 'Contorta') growing in my front yard. Any ornamental with such curious and contorted branches looks best when surrounded only by lawn, mulch, or ground cover.

Even though a contorted filbert tree appeals to my twisted sense of humor, it is definitely not the favorite of every visitor to the garden. Especially during the summer months, when the twisted leaves appear, visitors like to tell me that the tree looks wilted and is growing crooked. I tell them they're right: That's how the contorted filbert earned the name the "Politician's Tree." Angry taxpayers should suggest that a few crooked filberts be planted in Washington, DC, as a realistic alternative to all those straight-as-an-arrow cherry trees for which the place is famous.

The moral of this story has nothing to do with the morals of politicians. Rather, it is that unusual specimen plants look great when framed with empty space. No plant can compete with the twisted personality of the contorted filbert, and thus, it looks quite comfortable off by itself, a nonconforming loner in the landscape.

Weeping cherry trees, windswept pines, and trained or espaliered trees are other examples of artistic-looking plants that are used in show gardens as solitary focal points. Take a tip from the experts and surround these specimens with nothing but low-growing plants and empty space. Solitary situations are the best way to show off unusual forms. Sometimes less is best.

GOOD GROUND COVERS TO USE WITH SPECIMEN TREES

Obviously, there has to be something besides dirt surrounding the base of a specimen tree. Here are a few very low, nondistracting ground covers to blanket the ground beneath a specimen plant or tree. To really show off the shape of the tree, the ground cover or mulch should extend a foot or so beyond the drip line or branches of the tree.

Ajuga: ground cover for shade; is good beneath weeping trees or spring-blooming trees because it blooms in midspring

Ground-hugging junipers such as 'Wiltonii', 'Bar Harbor', and 'Blue Rug': take the sun; are good beneath large, rugged trees such as pine or spruce

Irish or Scotch moss: does well in sun or shade; is good tucked between boulders beneath a specimen in an Oriental-style garden

Pachysandra: an evergreen ground cover for shade; is good beneath large shade or woodland trees

Woolly thyme: low ground cover for sun; is good beneath bonsai

TYPES OF MULCH TO HIGHLIGHT A SPECIMEN TREE

Gravel mulch: Use for a more formal look. Pea gravel shifts around more and is more distracting than larger pieces of gravel or chipped rock. Be careful when using colored rock or red lava rock, as the color may distract from the plant you are trying to highlight. Inexpensive drainage rock — round, smooth, and about the size of a walnut — looks best under large evergreen trees or mature flowering trees, but smaller pieces of gravel can be used in very small areas, such as a clearing less than 5 feet wide with a dwarf, standard, or tree-form specimen.

Wood chip mulch: Bark or wood chips lend a casual, woodsy look and are a natural around needle-leaved evergreen specimen trees such as weeping cedar. Keep in mind that large chunks of bark are best for large areas around full-grown trees, but finely ground bark is best for small areas framing specimens less than 5 feet high.

A collection of large, smooth river stones: Flat stones give a contemporary/Oriental look to an area, so a mulch of this type is the perfect background for large, windswept pines and evergreens with a dwarfed or bonsai look. The sharp contrast between smooth river stones and the pointed blades of ornamental grasses is a visual feast that draws attention to unusual specimens that might otherwise go unnoticed.

FRAME IT WITH CONTRAST

Another way to showcase a splendid specimen plant is with the use of contrast. Let's say your favorite shrub has huge leaves. You might choose to plant something with tiny leaves nearby. For example, a large-leaved rhododendron may be set off by the contrasting texture of a fine-leaved azalea or kinnikinnick ground cover. (The addition of kinnikinnick to the landscape is always great fun because you now have an excuse to blurt out the nonsense-sounding but truly delightful word.) It's much more fun to use this common name rather than to call this evergreen ground cover by its botanical name, *Arctostaphylos uva-ursi*. If you want a little history to go along with this funny word, you can tell visitors that Native Americans used to smoke the tiny kinnikinnick leaves in their ceremonial pipes.

Leaves that are a contrast in size are not the only way to highlight plants. There are also contrasts in shape and form, contrasts in height, contrasts in color, and contrasts in leaf texture. As I write this, the flower border outside my window is blooming with a lovely example of contrast. A row of silvery-leaved dusty miller is planted behind a line of fibrous begonias with chocolate-brown foliage and bright pink blossoms. The colors make a sharp contrast, of course, but so do the finely toothed and pointed dusty miller leaves compared with the small, round begonia leaves. One has foliage with a texture that looks soft and furry, and the other has leaves so shiny and smooth that they appear wet. The begonias grow in mounds, whereas the dusty miller plants angle outward and upward with a more defined form. These are two very different-looking plants that make a beautiful display together. They are so opposite that the contrast is striking. Neither plant would have half the impact without the other one nearby.

CLASSIC CONTRASTS TO FIT YOUR STYLE

Formal/estate style: Clipped and stiff boxwood hedges contrast well with any of the casual-looking herbs or tall, old-fashioned flowers such as cosmos and feverfew, which is why boxwood makes such an effective border in American Colonial-style gardens. The straight edge of a boxwood hedge rigidly frames the loose sprawl of the plants growing in the center. Color contrasts, especially red and white, are popular in formal gardens. Perfectly manicured, dark green lawns look more formal when edged with white flowers.

Clipped evergreens and borders contrast with traditional flowers.

Country/cottage style: Tall, upright, and slender stalks of foxglove or hollyhock are a classic contrasting companion for bushy perennials such as peonies, daisies, or coreopsis. The Laurel-and-Hardy look is worth repeating often in any flowerbed. Just make sure that the tall, thin perennial is

Flowers with tall, slender stalks are classic companions for bushy plants.

grown in back of the short, fat plants. A contrast in flower shape and height is important in perennial beds because the planting is enjoyed as one unit, but the plants need to be arranged according to shape and size so they can all be seen.

Contemporary/Oriental style: Consider the fine needles and coarse look of a pine tree contrasting with the velvety smooth look of Irish or Scotch moss as a ground cover. Smooth river stones also make a pleasing contrast to the prickly needles of any evergreen tree or the finely detailed leaves of a Japanese maple. The use of space is very important in

Fine-needled evergreens and boulders are striking together.

the contemporary/Oriental style. The contrast of light and dark created by plant forms and shadows is a result of open space around plant groupings. Remember that the contrasts in textures more than in colors create the interest in this garden style.

Naturalistic/woodland style: Feathery ferns and shiny-leaved rhodies contrast nicely with the texture of tree bark. The white bark of the birchs provides an especially effective contrast.

White birch bark is an effective contrast for ferns, mosses, and other forest greenery.

Mediterranean/desert style: Stiff and prickly cacti or ornamental grasses look great with the cool, smooth surfaces of large boulders. Perhaps the most satisfying contrast of all is the sound of splashing water from an outdoor fountain on a sun-drenched terrace. Overhead vines and other structures that cast shadows also make pleasing patterns of contrast in bright sunlight.

Prickly cacti stand out when surrounded with smooth stones.

Opposites look attractive together no matter what style of garden you have. Choosing plants with different shapes, textures, and sizes are a few of the many tricks expert designers use in the most beautiful gardens of the world. Along with these contrasts in plant forms comes a more obvious design trick — contrasts in colors.

CONTRASTS IN COLORS

Let's take a mental vacation for a moment and imagine a country scene in Holland. Do you see red and yellow tulips blooming in front of windmills? The color contrast of red and yellow is a garden classic. A quick way to come up with flashy color combos is to picture in your mind the most memorable flower gardens you've driven past or visited. You usually remember what you liked best. Another shortcut to beautiful color combinations is to imitate the color groupings you see in garden picture books and to take note of pleasing combinations as you tour show gardens.

The list of color contrasts that follows was voted on by my favorite group of gardeners. These are the beautiful memories of the garden club women of Washington State. When I started writing a weekly garden column, it was the garden clubs that first invited me to their meetings as a guest speaker. After my talks, I answered plant questions and soon realized that among the 25 to 30 women present, there were experts from just about every facet of horticulture. One woman had been growing and breeding roses for 50 years, another was an experienced herb grower, and many more knew about perennials, lawn care, and bonsai. It was like sipping tea with a bookshelf of talking plant encyclopedias.

What makes these knowledgeable women different from the experts at plant symposiums and county extension meetings is their vast personal experience. In general, the garden clubbers are older, more experienced, and more open-minded about the knowledge they share. Sometimes "experts" (myself included) view gardening as a science. Logical people think there must be a scientific explanation for every success and failure in the garden and a right and a wrong way to solve gardening problems. Real garden lovers, who learn about growing from decades of dirty fingernails and weekends of wearing out gloves, treat gardening as an art, not an exact science. Plants may die because they don't like you or your yard. Rare flowers may bloom because you took the time to worry about them, not because of any special fertilizer you tried. There is a lot more openness to new ideas and innovative solutions to problems when gardening is practiced as a life-style or an art form instead of as a horticultural science to be dissected and studied.

Most of the clubs that I have spoken to are run by women who have been on their knees in the dirt for more than 40 years. They share their experience with confidence and joy. This is why I decided to poll garden club members to find out what they consider the showiest plant combinations. I asked them simply to remember a group of plants or flowers that had lodged in their memory as especially compatible and attractive. These are the flower, tree, and shrub combinations they found to be the most memorable.

Favorite Color Combinations of Bedding Plants and Annuals

Clear yellow marigolds and sky-blue pansies. This combo is best in a sunny area, for the sake of the marigolds, but not against a hot south- or west-facing wall, or the pansies will fade. Use any height of marigold, but the tall, big-headed marigolds give a more formal look than the short "lemon drop" variety. I have used this pair alongside a pathway with good results, but if you try to grow marigolds and pansies in the same pot, either the pansies dry up and fade too soon or the marigolds get too much water and produce fewer flowers. Both of these annuals can handle less-than-perfect soil, although the pansies demand added organic matter if the soil is on the sandy side.

Pink wax begonias with chocolate-brown leaves planted in front of silvery dusty miller. This is one of the most pleasing examples of contrasts in color, shape, form, and texture. Both plants are drought tolerant if given plenty of water until fully established. This duo makes a splash in full sun or partial shade. The fibrous begonias also bloom in full shade, but the dusty miller gets leggy without half a day of sun.

Bright red geraniums and white alyssum. Here's a color contrast perfect for pots and window boxes and sharp enough for even the most formal garden. Both need sun at least half the day, but you'll have blooms even if the soil is poor. Geraniums and alyssum both hate damp feet, so don't overwater, and provide good drainage. If you fuss over a perfectly maintained lawn, this combination makes a dashing border to frame your patch of green perfection. Put the low-growing white alyssum next to the lawn, with the taller geraniums in the back.

Yellow daffodils and blue grape hyacinths. This is the springtime version of yellow marigolds and blue pansies. The bright yellow daffodils must remind everyone of sunshine and the blue grape hyacinths of summer skies. The only problem with this classic is that sometimes the daffodils bloom before the grape hyacinths, and spring bulbs have a notoriously short bloom time. You can always cheat and plant daffodil bulbs in decorative pots of delft blue or use bright yellow flowers close to the painted blue trim of your house.

Pink geraniums and variegated ivy or green-and-white creeping Charlie. Most respondents remembered this combo growing from window boxes or spilling from hanging baskets, and in such cases, ivy geraniums were used instead of the common geranium. The clear pink and white with green is a very romantic color scheme that looks great in country gardens. Give these plants a sunny location and keep the ground cover of ivy or creeping Charlie under control with frequent pinching back during the growing season.

Hanging baskets with purple petunias, pink ivy geraniums, and blue lobelia. These colors are most admired in hanging baskets growing in the sunshine, probably because the pastels are so cooling on a summer day. The purple and lavender petunias are also very fragrant, and some gardeners noted that fact when reminiscing about this beautiful color combination. The blue lobelia comes in dark blue, medium blue, and light blue, but the particular shade didn't seem to matter to them as much as the pink, purple, and blue tones. Keep the petunias in any hanging basket well pinched back, or they'll smother the less ambitious lobelia. Grow this basket of color close to a water faucet, as lobelia is a thirsty plant.

THREE SEASONS OF BLOOMS IN 3 FEET OF SPACE

Here's a simple planting plan to fill a 3-foot-wide garden bed with three seasons of perennial color.

Plant daffodils in the back of the bed, bearded irises in the middle, and roses in the front. The daffodils bloom in early spring, when neither the dormant irises or pruned roses have foliage enough to block them from view. The iris leaves fill in to shield the dying daffodil foliage in late spring, and once the iris blooms fade away in June, the roses take over and provide summer-long color. The blue-gray foliage of the irises serves as a great backdrop for the roses during the summer months. (Choose shrub roses if you want mass color, hybrid tea roses for a more formal look.)

All the plants in this bed require good drainage, so consider raising the planting area by adding topsoil and using bricks, rocks, or landscape timbers as a border to hold the soil in place. All bloom the first year and will return to bloom again and again. Dig and divide the iris and daffodil bulbs every few years, or when the number of flowers begins to diminish. All three plants need at least half a day of sun but thrive in full sun as long as the roses are given ample water in summer.

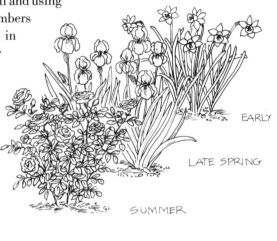

EARLY

LATE SPRING

SUMMER

Red geraniums, white petunias, and blue lobelia. This color scheme always flags down patriotic smiles. Most memorable was seeing these flowers blooming around a flagpole or a mailbox. The best arrangement is to have red geraniums near the back, white petunias in the middle, and blue lobelia in a border. Don't attempt this planting combination unless you have an area with good soil and full sun. Use the upright lobelia 'Crystal Palace' rather than the trailing 'Blue Cascade' for a display growing in the ground. Petunias should be the multiflora varieties, which are more compact and uniform for bedding displays than the grandifloras. A dependable white multiflora petunia is 'White Satin'. To make this flowerbed truly unforgettable, poke small American flags among the flowers on the Fourth of July.

Favorite Color Combinations of Trees and Shrubs

Pink and yellow. Pink-blooming trees such as flowering cherry, plum, or peach (the *Prunus* spp.) or pink dogwood *(Cornus florida)* are planted with yellow tulips or daffodils underneath. This combination is especially effective if the trees are planted in a row (for example, to line a driveway).

White and orange-red. White flowering trees or shrubs such as bridal wreath *(Spiraea)*, magnolias, or apple trees are underplanted with orange-red flowers such as tulips, poppies, or azaleas. Most of the showy ornamentals that are covered with white blossoms tend to bloom in spring, so it is sometimes difficult to pull this one off because spring bulbs and perennials have such short bloom times and the weather influences the exact date of their flowering. Still, the color contrast of orange and white is so striking that it's worth the weather gamble. A dozen orange-red tulips planted next to a spiraea or an arrangment of 'Hino' crimson azaleas around a magnolia tree makes beautiful sense.

Yellow and blue-purple. Yellow bloomers like forsythia or the golden chain tree (*Laburnum* x *Watereri*) with purple or blue flowers planted nearby. Hyacinths, purple crocuses, and purple primroses are the early bloomers that look best with forsythia, and the later-blooming golden chain tree looks spectacular with a blooming blue ground cover of *Vinca minor* or ajuga. Both of these yellow bloomers need frequent pruning to keep them looking tidy, and the golden chain tree should be protected from very hot summer sun. Parents of small children avoided the golden chain tree in the past because of its reputation as a poisonous plant. Actually, only the dried seedpods are toxic, and these can be removed from this small tree immediately after it blooms, giving more energy to the plant and less worry to the owners. Once again, it is the classic sunshine-and-blue-sky color theme that makes people remember this plant grouping as especially attractive.

Purple and gray. Trees and shrubs with purple foliage such as the blireiana plum (*Prunus* x *blireiana*), purple smoke tree *(Cotinus coggygria)*, or crimson-leaved anything are striking when surrounded by shrubs with gray or silver foliage, such as dusty miller, lavender, or artemisia. Never underestimate the

PLANNING AN EVENING PATIO GARDEN
WITH COLOR AND FRAGRANCE

At dusk, the colors in a garden change, and fade into the shadows. Not only do white flowers show up more at night, but they tend to be the most fragrant flowers you can plant. It's no coincidence that some flowers have a scent only at night. The white color and sweet scent is nature's way of attracting moths to do the nighttime pollinating. Many of these night-flying moths are as lovely to watch as the butterflies that flit about during the day.

Use flowering vines as a backdrop for your evening patio garden. Choose the fragrant night-blooming jessamine *(Cestrum nocturnum)* if you live in a freeze-free zone or the hardier honeysuckle if your climate is cooler; both vines have flowers that release a scent as the temperature cools at night. Wisteria is another great vine to add shade to a patio, and if you plant a white wisteria vine ('Alba'), you'll be rewarded with fragrance along with the fine, fat clumps of blossoms. In the beds near your patio, include heliotrope, dianthus, and flowering tobacco *(Nicotiana alata)*. Be sure to insist on the white varieties of these three for maximum fragrance as well as evening color. The 'White Lady' heliotrope fills the air with perfume at night.

In pots next to windows, decorate your fragrant evening garden with Madonna and Asiatic lilies. The scent is so strong when the buds open that they can easily be enjoyed indoors on summer nights just by opening a window. Both of these large-blooming lilies can be grown in pots but need to be stored in a garage or cellar if you have cold winters.

There are also annual flowers with scents and evening appeal, especially the purple-veined but lavender-colored 'Sugar Daddy' petunia. You'll always keep these petunias well pinched once you learn that the pruning leftovers can be brought indoors for long-lasting, fragrant bouquets.

Finally, find a little patch of ground near the patio for sweet peas. The old-fashioned climbing sweet peas perfume the evening air better than the modern knee-high varieties. Suspend some twine from the roof overhang and let the fragrant vines scramble up the side of the house, making a floral curtain for any windows in the way. Viewing the blossoms right outside the window also reminds you to be a loyal sweet pea plucker. As with garden peas, the more you pick, the more you get. Growing sweet peas and other blooming vines as a wall on one side of your deck or patio also provides you with privacy, shade, and wind control.

power of the foliage to provide the color contrast rather than the flowers. The purple-and-gray color scheme is practical in drought-resistant gardens because plants with gray foliage tend to be water misers, and both the purple smoke tree and purple-leaved plum can adapt to dry weather conditions.

Background Colors

Another way to use color contrasts to liven up your landscape is to consider the background color provided by your house, fence, or hedge. Drive through a residential neighborhood and notice how red geraniums look brighter when planted near a light gray house, compared with their dullness when used close to a home stained dark brown. This is why the charm of a white picket fence is so effective. It is not the use of white alone that dresses up the landscape, but the way plants and flowers seem to sparkle when white is used as a contrasting background color.

This doesn't necessarily mean that white is the best color to paint a house as a background to show off flowers. Some plants look better against a gray or earth-tone background. Beauty is definitely in the eye of the beholder, but if you want a garden that appeals to the most people, consider the following safe and appealing background colors.

White background. Use clear, bright colors (clear pink, bright red, clear yellow) with a white house, fence, shutters, or window box. Pink petunias, yellow marigolds, and bright red geraniums make a great color grouping in front of a white fence or dripping from planters or window boxes in front of a white house. Formal gardens, country gardens, and American Colonial gardens are usually shown with lots of white trim and blooming flowers with bright colors.

Gray or blue background. Use soft pastels such as lavender, blue, soft pink, and purple with a blue-gray house, gray stone house, weathered gray fence, or lots of gray cement or gravel in the yard. Romantic gardeners who love the touch of old-fashioned roses and worn stone benches may be drawn to pastel color schemes. Try pots of sky blue lobelia, lavender petunias, and pink or salmon begonias. The neutral gray of rocks or cement makes a great background for any color, but soft pastels blend well with a gray background to make the most harmonious color scheme. An all-white flower garden looks wonderful around a gray house with white trim.

Gold or yellow background. Use warm earth tones such as gold, orange, and cream with a gold or brown house, a brick path, or a brick house. Earth colors and brick exteriors look great with touches of creamy white alyssum and terra-cotta pottery. Sun-loving gardens with a Mediterranean/desert theme often have cream-colored adobe or brick walls. This type of background is perfect for showing off the warm gold, bright pink, orange, and red tones of sun-loving plants. Daylilies, golden poppies, calendulas (pot marigolds), and orange and salmon geraniums are naturals for bringing warmth to a golden background.

Single-Color Themes

Color contrasts are not the only way to make an impressive statement with the flowers and foliage in your garden. Some of the most beautiful show gardens in the world are known for their single-color themes. Examples are rose gardens in shades of pink, herb gardens using only gray foliage, and blue theme gardens with rich blue blossoms against a green background.

This reminds me of the night I enjoyed the most spectacular use of color I have ever seen in a suburban neighborhood. It was a summer evening, and while I was walking to my car after a meeting in an unfamiliar neighborhood, I was moonstruck. But unlike the Italian fable, it wasn't by love. Across the street was a modest home lit up by white flowers. The white blooms bordered the dark green lawn and flowed from pots that marched up the front steps. There were white flowers spilling from the window boxes on either side of the door. There was even a clump of white petunias and geraniums glowing in the moonlight next to the mailbox. The couple that tended this pristine landscape were as full of storybook charm as their surroundings: they had chosen an all-white color scheme in honor of their fiftieth wedding anniversary. The senior sweethearts had even repeated their wedding vows surrounded by friends, family, and a host of white perennials and annuals from their very own garden. (This story should inspire you to add a little drama with a single-color theme, to garden with your spouse, and to hang in there until your fiftieth wedding anniversary.) The all-white color scheme is also a wonderful choice for gardeners who come home late at night. There's no need for porch lights, as the moon's reflection on an all-white flower garden can light up the neighborhood.

This seems a fitting time to mention another white flower that positively glows at night. Candytuft *(Iberis sempervirens)* is a low-growing rockery plant covered with white blossoms every spring. Use it as a border alongside a walkway, and you'll have a path that lights up the neighborhood every night of the bloom season. A rockery full of flowering candytufts is definitely a showstopper.

WHITE BLOOMERS FOR DEEP SHADE

White flowers are very effective in deeply shaded areas where dark colors tend to fade into the shadows. A shaded or north-facing deck or patio feels lighter and brighter even on cloudy days just by choosing white and pastel flowers. Put the blooming plants in pots or hanging baskets so that they will be closer to eye level, and you'll lighten up the dark corners even more. Following are some white flowers that bloom in shade:

Fibrous begonias

'Lady' varieties *Impatiens*

Lobelia, both the trailing and upright 'White Lady' varieties

Tuberous begonias

Variegated-foliage plants (lots of white in the leaves) also do well and show up well in the shade. Following are some examples:

Ajuga reptans 'Variegata'

Caladium bicolor

Coleus hybrids

Hosta undulata

How to Showcase Families of Plants

If you have quite a few special plants that seem a little lost in the crowded underbrush, consider organizing your garden space into special families. You may remember from Chapter 1 that this was the solution to my own hodgepodge collection of plant favorites.

When we moved from our first home to a bigger piece of property, I brought with me some of my favorite plants from our first garden. With 2 acres of ground to plant, I had to make some quick decisions about what to plant where. Out of desperation, I planted all the rhododendrons and azaleas together in a group where they would be protected from the hot sun. To lessen the confusion, I planted all the pink bloomers near each other, then the reds, the whites, and so on. We added a path of stepping-stones so the plants would be easier to water, and, of course, one plant led to another. This garden of convenience became the start of our rhododendron garden.

I chose the spot for the rhodies because it had the moist soil and filtered sunlight that rhododendrons love. The grouping of similar plants together made it easier to care for them. It is certainly more convenient to water all the rhododendrons in one spot in summer and fertilize them as a group in spring.

The idea of family or like groupings of plants worked so well that we repeated the idea throughout our yard. The herbs are grown in a wheel design, the roses are in a more formal arrangement close to the house, and the perennials are loosely grouped into one section each for peonies, daylilies, and bearded irises. This makes an impressive splash of color whenever a particular plant is in bloom. Each spring, instead of murmurs of rhodie blooms throughout the garden, my rhododendron and azalea section shouts with a chorus of color. Of course, that particular area isn't full of color during the summer months, but that's when the rose garden has the spotlight. The iris section collects compliments in May but is ignored by visitors in July, when all they see are the mass plantings of daylilies, followed by the chrysanthemum and aster display in September.

Grouping families of plants together coordinates bloom times so that instead of a landscape with smatterings of color, you have the showier look of whole blocks of color. Your garden naturally evolves into a landscape that celebrates the seasons by having distinctive displays at different times of the year.

If all of this sounds familiar, it should, because it illustrates the pocket garden concept popular for many smaller gardens. You can really show off a collection of plants when they are grouped together and enjoyed as a chorus of blooms rather than as soloists. The more common the plant, the more important it is to do a mass planting. Consider how one blade of grass is ignored, but a billion blades together form a carpet of green that dominates every other plant form in the garden. Consider also how a dozen tulip bulbs sprinkled throughout a yard are barely noticed, but a dozen tulips blooming in one small area command center stage.

GETTING A SHOWCASE LOOK WHEN SHORT ON SPACE

Triple-Planting Bulbs for Longer Seasons of Color

Triple the length of time your potted bulbs bloom by planting three different types of bulbs at different depths in the same pot or planting hole. Choose a container that is at least 12 inches deep and has drainage holes. Add a few inches of soil, some bulbs, more soil, more bulbs, and so on. Think of it as flower bulb lasagna. The top layer should be the early bloomers, followed by midspring color and ending with the deepest-planted and largest bulbs, such as tall tulips.

You can also plant bulbs just two layers deep and put them directly in the ground, especially if you have a small garden. Just be aware that triple- and double-planted bulbs compete with each other for nutrients the following year and may not return to bloom again with as much vigor. Bulbs that have been layered may need to be treated as annuals and discarded after one season. Following are some suggestions for bulb layers:

Top layer: Early-blooming small bulbs can be planted just a few inches deep. These include crocus, windflower *(Anemone blanda)* and snowdrop *(Galanthus)* bulbs.

Middle layer: These bulbs are larger and bloom later in spring, so they can be planted a few inches deeper than the top layer (5 to 6 inches below the surface). Hyacinths, rock garden tulips such as 'Red Riding Hood', and daffodils can go in this middle layer.

Bottom layer: Tall, late-spring tulips such as the lily-flowered varieties or orb-headed allium bulbs can be planted deep into the ground, below the first two layers (about 8 to 10 inches below the surface). This last layer blooms just in time to hide the fading flowers from the earlier bloomers. Don't be shy about cutting back the early bloomers once they have finished flowering if you plan on treating these bulbs as annuals.

Show Plants by the Season

If you don't have a collection of plants to pull together into an organized display, build your own seasonal garden around a colorful tree or shrub. Use these steps as a guide to welcoming a season with color:

1. Choose a tree or specimen plant to use as a focal point. Let's use a fall garden as an example. A great tree to use as a fall focal point is a relatively inexpensive vine maple *(Acer circinatum)* or a more refined Japanese maple *(Acer palmatum)*.

2. Group three to five shrubs around the base of your main tree. The idea here is to choose a shrub that best complements the tree when it is at the height of its seasonal glory. If you use a vine maple as your main tree, grouping three burning bushes *(Euonymus alata* 'Compacta') around the maple means that the shrubs will be covered with brilliant red foliage in midfall, the same time that the vine maple is turning yellow and orange. (Give yourself a pat on the back if you realize you've just planted a complementary color scheme.) Any medium-size shrub that shows color at the same time as the focal point tree works well.

3. Finish the scene with a low-growing ground cover of blooming flowers. The fall garden we created in the first two steps would look lovely with a cotoneaster ground cover. This evergreen vine sports bright red berries in fall that complement the burning bushes and vine maple. The use of three types of plants with contrasting colors, heights, and shapes makes sense when planning seasonal gardens.

A list of showy trees and compatible shrubs with coordinated bloom times is difficult to compile. That's because Mother Nature does not cooperate by having everything bloom at the same time every year across the United States. She does insist that the show must go on, but she has never set a dependable time for the blooming curtain call. In some parts of the country, the cherry trees bloom in March, in others April, and in still others May. In the desert states, you wouldn't use a cherry tree for color at all.

The practical way to coordinate bloom time is to drive through a residential neighborhood, show garden, or public park when your own favorite tree is looking its best. Take note of what else is showing some color and the plants that would best enhance your bloomer at home. Don't rely on plants in bloom at the nursery, as these may have been trucked in from another area.

My neighbor with a weeping cherry tree made the mistake of checking a nursery instead of the neighborhood for an azalea to bloom in tandem with his lovely tree. He was very proud of the pink blossoms that showered the tree each April and decided to plant a few white azaleas nearby to emphasize the delicate cherry blossoms. A quick trip to the nursery produced three blooming azalea plants that he tucked into the soil around the blooming cherry. The effect was smashing the first spring. The mistake wasn't obvious until the following year, when the azaleas bloomed earlier than the cherry tree and were covered with nothing but faded brown blossoms when the buds began to break open on the weeping cherry. Had he looked across the street, he would have noticed a later-blooming azalea variety with buds just beginning to open. He also had lavender heathers and purple primroses growing in his backyard, and these would have complemented the cherry tree nicely.

Moving plants around so that they complement one another is a very practical way to get more beauty out of your landscaping budget and to accent your most attractive plants. The next time something blooms in your yard, scan the landscape for companion plants that are also putting on a show. You'll get plenty of applause if you let the smaller performers play backup to the big stars of the garden. These little bloomers will be drawn out of the shadows of your garden when they can share the spotlight with the serious contributors that usually stage a show all their own.

Building a garden spot that shines in a certain season takes observation of fine details. The joy comes in developing a garden with year-round interest instead of drowning in the typical spring splash and then thirsting for color the rest of the year. Make an effort to visit nurseries and garden centers during the dry months, and you'll meet plants you've never noticed before. Even the tiniest red berries from a shrub with winter interest are appreciated in a garden that usually shows color only in the spring and summer months.

Label Your Plants for Instant Prestige

The quickest way to shove any landscape plant into the spotlight is to label it. You don't need to have a garden full of those annoying plastic plant tags to give your yard a professional look. A few well-placed and nicely done plant

A TRIO OF SHRUBS WITH WINTER COLOR

Red-twig Dogwood *(Cornus stolonifera)*

This wonderful shrub for wet spots brightens winter-weary days with its blood-red branches. Grow this multistemmed shrub as a screen property or as a filler in a low wet spot. A native dogwood, it survives in almost any part of the United States, even through the heat of southern California summers, if kept watered. It has a tendency to take over, so use a shovel to root-prune the main plant each spring. Tiny white dogwood flowers decorate the shrub in summer, but the foliage is not very attractive, and you'll look forward to fall when the leaves disappear to reveal the winter beauty of the colorful twigs.

Cotoneaster (*Cotoneaster* species)

There are many varieties of this adaptable evergreen. The lower-growing types, such as creeping cotoneaster *(Cotoneaster adpressus)*, make especially handsome ground covers under evergreen or specimen trees. Winter color comes from a fine supply of scarlet berries that stand out against the shiny green foliage. The red-and-green color combination is similar to the winter classic of green holly and red berries, but without the sharp edges and insect problems that holly is stuck with.

Wintergreen *(Gaultheria procumbens)*

Use this slowly spreading plant as a ground cover in woodland gardens or as a companion for rhododendrons and other acid-loving plants. In winter, the leaves stay deep green and shiny, and the large red berries are edible but taste strongly of mint. This plant is a native of the eastern United States, where Native Americans used the berries to make tea. You'll enjoy winter flavor as well as winter color with this easy-to-care-for plant.

identification signs add greatly to the credibility and prestige of your gardening skills. It doesn't matter if the plant you choose to name is as common as a juniper. (For all of you beginning gardeners, a juniper is a hard-to-kill, rather prickly evergreen shrub used to excess in many landscapes.) Just having that neat little signpost next to a plant is like awarding knighthood to a common chimney sweep. The plant is the same, but the title gives the peasant instant prestige.

Now, I happen to dislike juniper plants. It probably stems (and leafs and roots) from a traumatic childhood experience that I've buried deep in my subconscious. Maybe I was pushed into the prickly shrubs or forced by my brothers to retrieve basketballs from a juniper thicket. (My sisters and I try to blame all our personal faults, shortcomings, traffic tickets, and overdue library books on growing up with too many brothers.) But whatever the real reason, I still hadn't met a juniper plant I really liked until I visited the garden of an old friend who knew very well of my juniper prejudice. She had asked for help redoing her landscape, listened respectfully as I warned her about using the trite, always static common juniper in her design. I had brought my friend a very rare rose plant to kick off her garden remodeling, and her handy husband made a fine-looking nameplate for the rose that forced visitors to stop and admire the specimen. Labeling that rose was such a successful way to get people to slow down and take an interest in the developing garden that plant signs began to show up in front of a few other choice plants as the remodeling progressed.

One day, a hand-carved label was positioned in front of a group of junipers that my rebellious friend had planted in the dry soil beneath some fir trees. After reading the inscription, I knew that the sign was made to teach me a lesson. It said simply, "Common Juniper. It can survive in uncommonly lousy soil."

Reading that signpost next to the juniper grove taught me that there are no common plants, just plants in need of a better public image. In a difficult growing situation (such as under the shade of a tree), a common or boring plant that thrives is always more attractive than any blooming or colorful plant doomed to struggle and slowly die. It also shows that a title or label can add luster and shine to even the most tarnished reputation. So, make a sign for your unmown lawn and call it a Wildflower Preservation Meadow. (Just be sure the sign is large enough to be read from the sidewalk. You wouldn't want anyone stepping into your meadow just to get close enough to read it.) When the neighbors complain, reassure them that you'll try to be tolerant of the windblown seeds from their common turf grass that may happen to blow into your environmentally correct wildflower preserve.

The quality of the label or sign is important. I prefer freestanding plant signs (on stakes) that can be easily read. Garden centers and plant catalogs sell this version. Of course, the labeling of an entire section of the garden (the wildflower meadow, the rose garden, or the herb garden) with a wood-carved or etched sign means the sign should be larger than one you would use to label just a single plant. Signs are one garden accent you don't want to overdo, or your landscape could end up looking like a retail nursery instead of a garden. Use labels to identify plants that are unusual or special and signs to illustrate a point or introduce a separate section of the yard.

Show Off a Garden with Lighting

Dusk can be a beautiful time to show off a garden, especially if weeds, a shaggy lawn, or other minor imperfections detract from its daytime beauty. Start your night life by focusing an outdoor light on your favorite focal point or specimen plant, then outline pathways and shrubbery with low-voltage light sources. Your yard will literally light up the neighborhood, especially on long winter evenings. It'll be like having holiday lights up all year long. Speaking of holidays, you can easily change the color and mood of your low-voltage lights simply by slipping a colored silicone sleeve over the bulb. This is a lot easier than hauling out the ladder to string traditional holiday lights.

Adding outdoor lighting does not have to be the escapade with underground wires and fuse boxes that it once was. Simple solar-powered light sources mean that even the electrically inept can do it themselves.

My husband loves to purchase different types of lights for our garden almost as much as he loves to buy noisy power tools and heavy bags of ready-mix cement, but this doesn't mean our yard is lit up like a helicopter landing pad. We do have a few easy-to-install, solar-powered lights in place (there's a lesson to be learned from this), but the low-voltage lighting sets that require digging and laying of wires are still in their boxes waiting to be installed, stockpiled in the "treasure shed" we maintain. The "treasures" (I am not allowed to call any of it junk) currently include a minimountain of broken bricks (waiting to become a brick planter), along with several sets of outdoor lights (innocent victims of procrastination) and a 10-year supply of powdered cement in bags that my husband stores in case a worldwide hardware shortage creates an acute lack of building materials at the same time he becomes desperate to build a new cement patio. Of course, this new patio will need to be surrounded with subtle but effective lighting, and all hardware stores could be permanently closed, so only those families (like ours) clever enough to have stockpiled building materials will get to spend the weekend working with cement and laying wire for outdoor lighting.

Unless you, too, have a large shed for storing light fixtures, broken tools, and useless lengths of wire, I urge you to buy solar-powered outdoor lights that can be installed quickly. They are available at any hardware store.

Lighting Directions

Backlighting, downlighting, and uplighting all refer to the direction in which the light source points. All can be used to highlight the specimen plants or anything else worth showing off in your garden.

Backlighting is the best way to cast shadows against a wall or give more depth to the landscape. To backlight a plant, simply aim the light behind the plant so that it casts a strong shadow onto the wall.

Use backlighting to illuminate the garden right outside your favorite window. Winter gardens are especially beautiful when maples, pines, and other plants with winter interest are backlit.

If you already use a floodlight or overhead light source, *downlighting* is how your garden is now lit. On a clear night with a full moon, anyone can enjoy the natural downlighting provided by Mother Nature. On moonless nights, a light positioned high in a tree or atop a post casts a similar spell on the garden. White flowers really sparkle when overhead lighting is used.

Uplighting is the best way to show off a spectacular specimen plant or focal point. Uplighting is when a light is directed upward at a taller object. Show gardens that offer evening tours use uplighting to showcase weeping trees, trees with interesting bark, and shrubs with strong lines.

The best plants to accentuate with lights are those with a good branch structure or an interesting shape. Ponds, fountains, and other water features are overflowing with nighttime drama that can be appreciated only with outdoor lighting. Contemporary/Oriental garden styles seem to make the best use of spotlighting trees and shrubs, but formal gardens can also gain a new dimension by lighting up statues, fountains, and solid walls.

Some of the world-class show gardens offer night tours that emphasize the use of outdoor lighting in the garden. If you visit a well-lit garden at night, you'll never again think of sunset as the end of your gardening enjoyment.

SUREFIRE SHORTCUTS

❖ Add a sign to your theme garden to give it instant prestige and identity.

❖ Use solar-powered lights to line the walkway to your front door.

❖ Choose a graceful tree or shrub close to the house and position a light source behind it to dramatize the branch patterns.

❖ Rip out the shaggy plants that surround your favorite specimen tree and replace them with a low-maintenance mulch of bark chips, smooth river stones, or ground cover plants.

❖ Pick up some annual flowers from the garden center, for example, easy-to-grow lemon-drop marigolds and sky-blue pansies or lobelia.

❖ If you have a tree or shrub with burgundy foliage, add a silver-leaved plant such as dusty miller, artemisia, or lamb's ears.

❖ Leave any large boulders you have inherited with the landscape. Mound soil around the giant rocks and plant a weeping evergreen tree or rustic pine between the protruding boulders on top of the mound.

❖ Don't hide your best-looking plants in an out-of-the-way corner. Consider transplanting any hidden specimens.

❖ Never underestimate the power of the pruning shears. Remove any crossing, broken, or weak inner branches and you may discover a prince of a specimen plant.

❖ Highlight a collection of plants by using three different forms of the same plant. A rose garden with climbing roses on a trellis in the background, hybrid tea roses in the middle, and low-growing minia-ture roses along the front border draws more attention than a tradi-tional rose garden of all hybrid teas. The same idea can be used with snapdragons and sunflowers. Many large mail-order seed companies sell snapdragons in tall, intermediate, and dwarf sizes; and sunflowers in 'Giganteus' (10 feet tall), large (5 feet tall), and dwarf (2 feet tall) sizes.

Most-Asked Questions about
Showcasing Show-Off Plants

Q. *I am putting in a new landscape and would like to use only especially beautiful plants, not the same old trees and shrubs that fill my neighbors' yards. But I am having trouble finding enough unusual specimen trees. I read about a lavender-blooming jacaranda tree, but none of the nurseries around here have even heard of it! Why do all the nurseries and garden centers sell the same old things, and where can I find some unique plants for my garden?*

A. Variety may spice up your landscape, but if the unusual plants you want can't survive in your climate, you won't find them for sale at your local nursery. The lavender jacaranda tree you're hunting for is frost tender and cannot survive in a cold-winter zone. It is more important to design a landscape using plants that thrive in your area than it is to acquire plants just for the sake of novelty. The plants that are doing well in your neighbors' yards and that are available at the local nursery are the tried-and-dependable varieties. Visit an arboretum or city park and take note of any unusual specimens that have survived to maturity. You may then be able to ask any large garden center to special-order the trees that you want. Or you can hunt through the mail-order catalogs and order by mail.

There is another way to tell whether a plant will survive in your area. The U.S. Department of Agriculture has assigned a climate zone to each part of the country, and these numbers are often indicated after a plant's description. There are 11 hardiness zones, ranging from Zone 1, the coldest parts of Canada, to Zone 11, which is almost frost free. Check the North American Hardiness Zone Map to find out exactly which zone you garden in, and you'll have some guidelines by which to determine which unusual plants can survive in your climate.

Q. *We are landscaping our first home on a strict budget and can't afford any expensive specimen trees or shrubs. We inherited most of the plants when we bought the house, and they look healthy enough, but there's nothing very special about any of them. They are mostly evergreens and a few flowering shrubs. What can I plant to add some sparkle to our boring landscape without spending a fortune?*

A. If you have a good frame of healthy, but common, trees and shrubs, you can enjoy an exciting landscape by adding drama with bulbs, annuals, and perennials. Prune back or de-limb any overgrown evergreens to allow more light into the garden beds and to make more room for the seasonal displays of color. Bulbs and perennials are especially attractive to the thrifty gardener because they are an investment that multiplies with each division and returns blooming dividends each year.

Q. *I'm putting in a rose garden and having a difficult time making up my mind about which are the most beautiful varieties. What rose do professional designers consider the most beautiful?*

A. Unless the professional designer lives at your house, there is no need to choose plants that somebody else thinks are beautiful. Most gardening professionals rate their favorite plants according to whatever happens to be in bloom at the time or whatever looks the healthiest. When it comes to roses, red is the color most often ordered from a florist, but not the most popular one to grow. In general, red roses are less disease resistant than pink roses, and their color fades more quickly in the sun. The bicolor 'Peace' rose is considered by many as the gardener's favorite, not only because of its lovely peach-yellow but also because of its large bloom size, disease resistance, and cold hardiness.

Chapter Summary

❖ Accentuate the best in your garden by showcasing the great-looking specimens.

❖ Call attention to great trees and shrubs by framing them with open space and using contrasts in textures, sizes, and colors.

❖ Consider the color of your house or other background when choosing color for the landscape. Pastel colors look best against gray backgrounds; clear colors sparkle against white.

❖ Single-color themes can be very effective. White flowers are especially beautiful at night.

❖ Group families of plants together for seasonal displays. For example, arrange all the spring bloomers in one corner and the fall color in another section. By doing so, you consolidate the blooms for a showy splash of color.

❖ Use garden lighting to put the spotlight on your special specimen plants.

CHAPTER 6

Showcase Your Design with Walls, Borders, Paths, and Arches

SHORTCUT:

Outlining the boundaries in your garden by using borders, paths, and walls is a quick route to a clean, finished, and dressed-up look.

Remember when you were learning how to color? You filled in the spaces very carefully, followed all the rules, and colored in only one direction, but the picture never looked quite finished until you learned how to outline. Just using a darker color to trace over all the borders made everything look neat, clean, and orderly.

Outlining the borders in your garden design is a finishing touch that improves the look of your whole landscape. Defining the edges of paths and perimeters in your garden is a shortcut to neatness. If you want to tidy up your yard in a hurry and give it the crisp, clean look of a showcase garden, remember to outline. Start by using strong lines for your borders and paths. To dress up these boundaries quickly, accent them with arches, walls, fences, and screens.

Garden Walls: Fences, Shrubs, and Screening

We've all seen the instant transformation that occurs in a small backyard when a solid wood fence is built on the property line. The feeling of openness and exposure changes, the sense of space is different, and even the light becomes more diffused. Adding a fence or other type of barrier is the most effective way to define your outdoor space.

There are many practical reasons to fence in a space — for privacy, pet control, kid security, or a windbreak, to name just a few. But, don't let these practical functions detract from the charm or style of your landscape.

Adding boundaries to your garden can give the landscape an instant showplace look by establishing separate garden rooms or sections. Think about how walls in a home separate the formal dining area from the family room. If your home has an open floor plan, there is a more casual feeling. If your dining area is in a separate room enclosed on all four sides, it becomes more boxed in but also more formal. The walls themselves are not as important as what they do to the space. Now, transfer this theory to your outdoor living area. If your backyard patio and open grassy area are separated by a low hedge or brick wall, it makes both areas feel smaller, the same way that adding a wall between a kitchen and family room does; but, it also makes both spaces feel more intimate and formal, just as eating meals in a separate room elevates the act of nourishment to a dining experience.

HOW WALLS ARE USED IN SHOW GARDENS

The designers of show gardens and large public parks break outdoor space into smaller garden rooms all the time. Part of the excitement of visiting a very large estate or show garden is the movement from one theme garden to another. Hedges, fences, and other barriers keep the viewer from being able to see all of what is coming next. These visual barriers turn open space into separate rooms.

Of course, you probably don't have the space or the inclination to break up your own property into individual gardens, but anyone with a yearning for a formal/estate-style landscape should realize that adding a few outdoor walls can be a shortcut to that formal feeling.

WALLS AND BORDERS IN HOME GARDENS

A good example of what a low garden wall can do to a home landscape is the way a boxwood hedge around a rose garden changes the look. Outlining any garden bed with a low hedge gives it a formal, tidy look.

Now, imagine a lawn outlined with a brick or cement border. Even a rather thin, sickly lawn looks impressive when curbing, landscape timbers, or a brick mowing strip frames the green.

Formal gardens aren't the only places that can draw on borders and boundaries to add to the showplace look. The walled gardens of the English countryside, where thickets of roses, brambly hedges, and loose stone walls divide cottage gardens from one another, are legendary. If you love the casual, country look, using a low rockery or boundary of blooming shrubs can add to this easy-blooming country garden feeling.

Dividing the space into a more intimate area can also add to the serene and peaceful feeling of a contemporary/Oriental garden. If there is traffic or other noise to block out, a screen planting or wooden fence can block the view and help limit how much the eye can see and the ear can hear. Remember that the Eastern influence on landscaping has taught us that less is more. Less background view gives more weight to the plants and vistas within the garden.

Even the Mediterranean/desert-style landscape needs walls and boundaries. Imagine a sunny courtyard with the added embellishment of a low brick or tile wall on which to sit. Every garden style can be enhanced by some type of boundary. The trick is to add the right type of wall or screen in the right location so that the space is contained but not boxed in. The goal is to put in enough boundaries and outlines to create a space that is intimate and private without making it seem cramped or small.

Introducing Pocket Gardens to Small Lots

If you have a lot of space to work with, the idea of separate outdoor rooms may sound attractive. If you garden on a lot that is average to small in size, the idea may take a little getting used to. In real life, the idea of breaking up your already-small space into even smaller sections is probably making you shudder with claustrophobia. Stop shuddering for a minute, and instead of thinking of garden rooms with different themes and different fence styles, try to think of your space as a collection of small pocket gardens.

Pocket gardening is the phrase I use to help homeowners organize their modest-sized lots into a series of separate garden areas. The pockets or planting areas are sewn together in the landscape using low borders and boundaries that define the gardens without stitching them permanently into the earth. If you really want to continue with the sewing metaphor, you can think of pocket gardening as a patchwork of minigardens with decorative stitches and nice wide borders at the perimeter. An ensemble of pocket gardens can look pieced together, but never as if it is about to unravel.

Creating Personal Pocket Gardens

When Joe and I bought our first home, it sat in the middle of a small lot surrounded by dirt and weeds. Only the driveway was roughed in. Time, money, and space were tight in those first years, and it was easier to think of the landscape as a series of small gardens (small enough to slip into our back pockets) that wouldn't cost a fortune (because we could spend only the money found in our back pockets).

The first pocket garden began as a rock garden around the base of a large fir tree with football-sized stones used for the border. This was a garden of convenience because we needed a spot to pile all the rocks from the yard and nothing grew under the fir tree anyway. It was a rock garden in the true sense of the word, inspired by the giant boulder left in the area by the builders. We weren't about to move a boulder as big as a car. Once again, frugality became the father of inspiration, and the giant boulder became the focal point of our first rock garden.

After building the rock garden, we started on a fern garden situated on the shady side of the house because wild ferns were already growing there anyway. We used a fallen log as the border in this rustic garden to outline the bed of moss that happily took the place of a high-maintenance lawn.

Another pocket of space became a tiny rose garden that was sandwiched in between the driveway and outlined with the more formal look of landscape timbers. The colorful annual garden that bordered the path to our front door was outlined with brick because this was the most formal part of the garden.

What made these separate areas seem like individual or pocket gardens were the borders and barriers that separated them. Traditional cement curbs, brick walls, and boxwood hedges aren't your only choices for garden borders. Tall, strong borders would have been too confining in our small front yard. The borders or walls that defined our pocket gardens were low, visual borders such as railroad ties, rocks, bricks, and timbers. Not only are these types of borders quick to establish, qualifying them as real shortcuts, they're also inexpensive and easy for weekend garden warriors to add in an afternoon.

Now, let's get back to your own outdoor space and the different types of pocket gardens you would like to have. Have you been dreaming of an herb garden or a collection of roses? You don't need boxwood hedges or a white picket fence around your rose collection, even if you admire them in magazines. The public park may show off its collection of roses with a brick wall enclosure, but in your pocket rose garden (perhaps six rose bushes are all you have space for), use a single layer of bricks to outline an octagon-shaped bed or a circular rose garden and separate the lawn from the rose bed. Put a path of stepping-stones on the rose bed leading to a sundial or other focal point in the center. Your small collection of roses suddenly looks like an impressive theme garden.

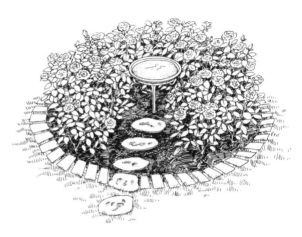

Stepping stones and an outline of bricks enhance any pocket garden.

If herbs are what you have in mind, lay a wooden wagon wheel on the ground and plant between the spokes (great for a desert-style garden), or try a fire fighter's garden with a ladder on the ground and the plant collection growing up through the slats. (See illustration on page 128.) One of the tidiest herb gardens I've ever seen was growing in the yard of a brick mason. He wasn't using bricks to define the herb beds, however. It was something much easier than that. The clay flue liners used inside chimneys were set up like bottomless terra-cotta pots, and each one held a different herb. Red rock lined the pathways between the red-colored tiles, which were arranged in neat, symmetrical rows. A large clay pot of tomatoes in the center turned this once-forgotten side yard into a convenient and attractive kitchen garden. The effect would have been entirely different without the heavy flue tiles forming such defined cubicles for the plants.

Easy-to-add low boundaries are great for separating small pocket gardens within the landscape, but for the perimeter of your property, you need more defined garden walls.

SEVEN TINY POCKET GARDENS

Herb garden: Compact herbs such as chives, dwarf basil, lavender, and oregano fit nicely into the openings of concrete blocks, wagon wheels, or ladders. Herbs need especially strong borders, as many of them spread quickly and sprawl.

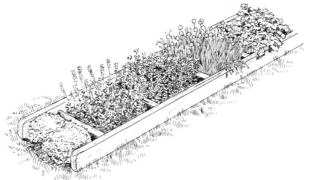

A ladder garden creates instant borders for herbs.

Mini-rose garden: Miniature roses with names such as 'Cinderella', 'Cupcake', 'Puppy Love', and 'Yellow Doll' can be bordered with a tiny 1-foot-high picket fence to form an enchanting rose garden.

Salad garden: A beautiful collection of red- and green-leaf lettuce, onions, kale, and edible violets can be grown in a salad bowl shape and edged imaginatively with old plates set on edge and half buried in the soil. One gardener even used recycled wine bottles, stuck into the ground upside down, to make an unusual green glass border.

Sedum garden: Sedums are succulent plants that thrive in sunny, well-drained spots. Hen and chickens is a common succulent that grows in a rosette pattern and can be used as a living border for a collection of stonecrop, gold moss, and cobweb houseleek *(Sempervivum arachnoideum).*

Cat lover's garden: Catnip is the ground cover in this garden, but because catnip *(Nepeta cataria)* is such a vigorous, spreading plant, you need a strong border. You can make one by intertwining twigs to form a solid fence with plastic edging sunk in the ground to prevent the spread of underground catnip roots. Match the branch fence with a twig shade structure or cat-sized tepee of branches. Leave a cat-sized opening in the twig enclosure, and your pet will spend many hours lounging in this garden, happily high on catnip.

A secret sunflower garden makes a perfect playhouse.

Secret children's garden: Many people build an area for children to play but never border it with anything other than some landscape timbers to keep the pea gravel or wood chips in place. Why not use a border of sawhorses for children to ride or a sturdy support for grapevines that children can also climb? A tepee covered with scarlet runner beans and a playhouse made of gigantic sunflowers are other whimsical ideas using plants that children love to grow.

Fern garden: Fallen logs and de-limbed tree branches make wonderful rustic borders for a fern collection. Sword fern, maidenhair fern, painted fern, and deer fern are all easy to grow in shaded, moist soil. Rocks, tree rounds set in the ground on edge, and even small stumps can be used to make borders between the ferns.

Walls around the Perimeter of the Garden

The walls or boundaries that define your property line are different from the ones that break up your yard into separate areas. Fences, hedges, and other barriers are much longer and broader than the row of bricks or timbers that outline the flowerbeds. This usually means a project that takes more than just a weekend's worth of work. I'm not about to call building a solid wood fence or planting a 20-foot hedge a shortcut. These are major investments in time and money. However, adding embellishments and improving your existing fence and hedge lines are the shortcuts that you can do in a weekend. With a little creative work, any boundary can become an addition to your landscape instead of just a division of the property.

BEAUTIFYING A BORING FENCE LINE

❖   Attach a feature. Nail a birdhouse, hang a half-basket, or add outdoor wall art to the bare section of a fence to direct the eyes toward that section. Plantings on either side of the focal point form a niche or alcove for the fence-hung feature. Choose plants that stay narrow if you want to frame a fence feature without hiding it with new growth. Skinny evergreens such as 'Pyramidalis' arborvitae or yew have the right shape to frame a fence feature.

Nail a birdhouse to your fence to create an instant focal point.

❖ Add a top piece. A section of lattice added to the top of a solid wood fence is the most common example, but carving the points of pickets and capping a stone or brick wall with flagstones are other ideas. You can also add a roof crest to give a solid fence an Oriental look.

❖ Break up the flat line by adding a gate and an arch. Gates and arches are becoming popular again as traditional-style homes and landscapes make a comeback. Remember, you don't have to put a gate only where you need one. If your family room window looks straight out on the backyard fence, add a decorative gate at that spot as a focal point in the fence line. You can even have a faux gate that doesn't have hinges to open. Just build a section in your fence 4 feet wide and embellish it with an archway or handle.

❖ Add wood or wire brackets and use your solid wood fence as a wall for hanging baskets of flowers. Fill the baskets with ivy for evergreen color; add annuals for summer color.

❖ If your fence is made of cyclone fencing material or any type of open wire, use it as a frame for growing vines. Climbing roses, ivy, nasturtiums, and honeysuckle are good vines for climbing a wire fence.

HOW TO ADD COLOR TO AN EVERGREEN AND EVER-BORING HEDGE

A static laurel or arborvitae hedge can come alive with color if you use the green background it provides to show off blooming shrubs positioned in front of the evergreen hedge. Following are some of the best shrubs to plant in front of an evergreen hedge:

Forsythia: A favorite for early-spring color, forsythia looks best when viewed from a distance and given a darker background such as a hedge planting. The darker the green of the hedge, the better the golden blooms stand out.

Hydrangea: Plant for summer color in a shady or sunny spot, and the huge hydrangea blooms can be enjoyed even from across the yard. This shrub does need frequent watering when in bloom, so be sure your hose or sprinkler system reaches the root zone.

Red-twig dogwood: The blood-red twigs stand out handsomely against an evergreen hedge or wooded background in winter. This spreading shrub thrives in wet spots, but be careful to keep the root system from invading the nearby hedge planting.

Star magnolia: This magnolia is a shrub, not a tree, and it blooms with fragrant white blossoms later in spring than forsythia. White stands out against any evergreen hedge.

Choose shrubs hardy enough to compete with the hedge for food, water, and sunshine. Try to locate any new plants at least 2 feet away from an established hedge to avoid digging into the root zone.

Perennial flowers such as daylily, peony, and iris also show up better when there is a solid background for display. Keep in mind that the soil near a hedge planting must be fertile and well watered to support the lush displays of perennial flowers you see in picture books. Amend the soil with manure, grass clippings, and compost before even attempting a perennial display near the root zone of a mature hedge.

TAKING A SHORTCUT TO A BEAUTIFUL FENCE LINE

Here's a tip that most homeowners forget: You only need one or two sections of fence or hedge in your front yard to make an impressive backdrop. Choose the fence of your dreams, be it a rustic split-rail or classic picket fence, then put in only 5 to 10 feet of the fence. Use this short section to screen the front door or to block off a front yard sitting area. The tiny section of fence is affordable, is the right style, and makes a perfect background and foreground for the plants you invest in.

FOUR STEPS TO BUILDING YOUR DREAM FENCE

A dream fence takes time and money. If you break the project into four steps, you're more likely to end up with the fence of your dreams.

1. Sink in the posts. Use cement to anchor the posts in the ground for a really strong fence. Connect them with a roll of wire fencing or bamboo screen to make a temporary barrier, if necessary.

2. Weeks or even months later, add the wooden slats or boards between the posts. These are called rails. They connect the posts and set up the framework for the slats or boards. Some fences are

One or two sections of fencing can make an impressive backdrop.

finished at this point, forming an open, casual fence line. Low fences, usually 3 to 4 feet tall, look fine with just the post and rails. You can make them of rustic cedar for a naturalistic/woodland garden or use finish wood, painted white for a formal/estate look.

3. Add the pickets or boards to the fence framework. This is when you decide whether you or your neighbor gets to see the "good" side of the fence or whether the slats are nailed on with every other one facing front.

4. Dress up the fence by adding wooden finials or light fixtures to the posts and applying the paint or stain.

Realistically, even building a dream fence in stages takes time and money, but if you want that showplace garden look, you need a wall or boundary with style. Remember you can build just three sections of your absolutely beautiful dream fence and use it as a screen.

FENCES, HEDGES, AND GARDEN WALLS FOR DIFFERENT GARDEN STYLES

Formal/estate style: Choose borders of wrought iron, brick pillars with wrought iron, solid brick walls, and clipped hedges of laurel, yew, or boxwood. Add a formal look to any fence by adding wooden finials to the fence posts.

Country/cottage style: Picket fences, solid wood with lattice on top, stone walls, and hedges of roses, lilacs, or other blooming shrubs. You can give any solid fence a more country look by purchasing ready-made plain pickets from the lumber store and taking them to a carpenter or wood shop for custom work on the points to give the curves and rounded tops seen on traditional picket fences.

Contemporary/Oriental style: Vertical-board fence lines, pole fences of bamboo, hedges of tall ornamental grasses or pine trees, and any fence or screen that uses the same siding material as the one on the house. This helps make a fence that is unobtrusive and in harmony with the building.

Naturalistic/woodland style: Log fences; trees, and native plants as natural borders; split-cedar or split-rail fences; medieval-style wattle fences; and loose rock walls.

Mediterranean/desert style: Split-rail fences, staggered tree planting, adobe walls, grape stake fences, cement block walls, and wagon wheels standing upright.

SCREENING INSTEAD OF FENCING

Often, all you need is a bit of privacy screening near the patio, not a full fence line. A showy shortcut you can borrow from Minter Gardens, a show garden in British Columbia, Canada, is to build a tall frame for a fence but hang baskets of flowers in the opening instead of using wooden slats or boards to fill in the space. What you are building is a fence on stilts. Place a line of potted plants under the hanging baskets that swing from this screen, and the pots will collect the drips from the overhead baskets.

If three sections of fence close to the patio or house seem like too much enclosure, make the first section tall, the middle section shorter, and the third section the lowest. Stair-stepping sections of a screen adds interest and cuts down slightly on the cost of materials.

Another way to turn a solid wood fence into a decorative screen is to build a dip or curve into the top. Once again, you may want to take your precut fence slats to a wood shop and have them cut at different lengths to make a graceful dip.

Toward a More Pleasurable Pathway

Garden paths do a lot for the structure, or bones, of a garden and lead the eye toward a vista. (If you're spooked by the term bones when landscape architects toss it around, remember that all it refers to are the lines, framework, or skeleton of the garden.) What really matters about the placement of pathways is getting to the garbage can without getting your slippers wet, or leading guests to the front door without losing them in the shrubbery. Once these basic needs have been met, it's easy to dress up the walkways and take steps toward more pleasurable-looking paths.

There is no need to enter the designers' debate on whether pathways should be straight and direct or curving and charming. That all-important path to your front door is probably already in place. (See Chapter 2 for ideas for enhancing the front entrance.) The shortcuts you should consider are ways to improve the look of the paths you have established.

There are ways to embellish or outline boring paths serving a needed function in the garden, just as you can dress up a plain fence. Depending on the garden style that most appeals to you, one of these tips might be just what you need to make your pathway a pleasure to view.

❖ Borders can tame the jungle look. Outline the borders with bricks or cement blocks on either side of a paved path to make it wider. If you have a casual pathway covered with wood chips or gravel, border it with rocks, landscape timbers, or fallen trees. Adding borders to your pathways is such an effective way to clean up a sloppy-looking landscape that sometimes it's all that's needed to change the look. I'm thinking of an older woman who moved into a house that had been vacant for more than a year. The backyard had turned into a jungle of overgrown shrubbery, and ivy had taken over the lawn. Other ground covers invaded the former flowerbeds, and weeds had become opportunistic, covering every other inch of this place. This new homeowner was a very practical woman. She realized that her budget would not cover the cost of all the pruning and hauling that would be required to turn the backyard jungle into the lawn-and-flowerbed landscape it had once been. She was also honest enough to admit that she had no time to keep up a standard backyard, had no use for a lawn, and was more than a bit partial to the natural green look that was joyfully covering her back property. The simple solution to this overgrown problem was to mow pathways through the plant life and use strong borders to define the paths.

❖ Formal borders of brick were used near the house to frame a gravel courtyard for outdoor furniture. Two paths led away from this courtyard, both bordered with landscape timbers that were laid down 4 feet apart over sheets of newspaper. Newspaper and cardboard sheets were used right on top of the ivy to form the pathways, and several inches of cedar shavings were piled on top of the cardboard weed block. The parallel lines of the landscape timbers kept the cedar shavings in place and discouraged the ground covers from reaching into the new pathway. Even ivy can be smothered by a thick layer of newspaper or cardboard with a liberal frosting of wood shavings on top to walk on. Gravel could also have been used as a pathway material.

❖ The backyard jungle was turned into a path garden, and maintenance was minimal. If the homeowner had wished to clear out the tangle of plants and turn it into a true garden, the project could have proceeded while the defined pathways made the backyard look presentable. In this case, she was interested only in trimming the green away from the paths and keeping the gravel courtyard free from weeds. The rest of her backyard was to be left as a wild habitat for the birds she loved to watch. By adding new paths and strong borders, she achieved those goals.

❖ Add pots on either side of the entry. Add more pots across from each other along the path to give a formal look, or stagger the placement of the pots to lend a more casual look.

❖ Plant dwarf evergreen shrubs, tree roses, or azaleas along the start or end of the path.

❖ Flower borders along the path are one of the most effective ways to dress up a walkway, but it takes a lot of flowers to fill in even a short pathway. Plant spots of color along the path instead.

❖ Dig holes deep enough to accommodate gallon-sized nursery pots next to your paths and pop already-grown flowers into the holes. You can change the flowers with the seasons: primroses in spring, annuals in summer, and potted mums in fall.

- ❖ Posts along the path connected with lengths of chain or rope make a simple but effective pathway railing.

- ❖ A low brick or stone wall or a fence that follows the line of the pathway echoes the shape and gives you a place to set pots or hang planters.

- ❖ Run a ribbon of gravel or loose stones along the border of the pathway to keep it clean and make it seem broader. Lay stepping-stones or bricks in the gravel to give the illusion of even more breadth.

- ❖ Add outdoor lighting next to the path, and you'll be grateful every evening.

Arches, Arbors, and Gates: An Impressive Welcome

Adding an arch to your outdoor world is the easiest, quickest route I know to a welcoming landscape. Once again, the romantic garden style of a country landscape usually comes to mind when a garden arch is mentioned. Don't be fooled into thinking that traditional homes and country gardens are the only styles enhanced by an arch. The styles discussed here are meant to show how any garden entryway can become an impressive statement.

If you need more evidence of how much an arch can add to a landscape, just take a look at the arches that grace show gardens and indoor display gardens. Many show gardens use archways, pergolas, and entry gates to separate one outdoor room from the next. An arch gives the visitor a feeling of welcome as she or he walks from one garden style to another. To tell you the truth, many of the arches illustrated here are copies of the designs actually used at these show gardens.

Before either panic or illusion sets in at the thought of such a lofty project as an arch, let me lead you in the direction of success by suggesting a very simple arch. I firmly believe that all those glossy photos of perfectly kept gardens you see in landscaping books scare off the average homeowner. The curving, 4-foot-wide arches, painted white with latticework up the sides, look impressive and difficult to build, and they are! And, the prebuilt arches you can find for sale at lumber stores may be more expensive than you can justify spending for garden ornamentation. But, there is a compromise. Building a simple archway over a path in your garden can be done in just a few hours for just a few dollars. I know, because that's exactly what my husband did one afternoon. To further assure you of the simplicity of the task, keep in mind that on this particular day, Joe was in charge of our three young children. He built the arch while the two younger kids napped, assisted in the project only by a 7-year-old.

The simple arch is best built with simple materials. You need four barn poles, two of them at least 10 feet long. Dig two parallel holes, sinking the tallest poles into the ground at least 2 feet deep. Fill in the holes with cement, if necessary, for added stability. The poles should be at least 4 feet apart. Now, notch the crosspieces with an ax so they rest snugly on the posts and join the butt ends at the top with glue or nails.

Matching flower pots can dress up a simple arch.

We also built a pergola, or pair of archways, for our wisteria vine, using the fallen alder trees on our property. Joe used a hatchet to de-limb the fallen trees, peeled off the bark, and then used the trees in their natural state. It's been 5 years and the poles show no signs of rotting, but I know we're pushing our luck. A second arch built from treated fence posts was just as easy to build but cost a bit more for materials. A third archway in our garden separates the formal front yard from the more informal backyard. This arch is made of finished wood with a design cut into the top plywood section with a jigsaw. It was a more complex undertaking than the simple afternoon project to build the first arch, but it adds to the formal look of the front.

Lest you miss the main advantage of building with peeled logs or treated fence posts, let me remind you that no maintenance is required on unpainted wood projects. An arch is one garden project that is easy to dress up without paint. Try one of the following enhancements for your simple arch:

❖ Hang blooming baskets from the ends of the crosspiece.

❖ Add corner brackets to the joints.

❖ Use vines such as wisteria or clematis to cover an arch that isn't pleasing to look at.

❖ Place twin pots of flowers or matching shrubs at the bottom of the arch to formalize and call attention to it.

❖ Hang house numbers or the name of your theme garden at the high point of the arch.

PLANTS FOR A SHOWCASE ARCHWAY

The big surprise here is that vines that ramble all over and cover your arch do not always grow to complement the structure. Romantic gardeners have to face the facts: Climbing roses bloom for only a few months and then make a point of looking dangerous and thorny the rest of the year; clematis has personality problems of a different type.

Most vines such as the clematis are enthusiastic growers, which means they can quickly swallow up the simple arch you have built and string out on their own in search of more structures to devour. When vines are used on arches, the look is often wild, informal, casual, and, let's face it, even messy (which isn't too strong of a description for a plant that is digesting an archway). Unless you promise to prune, tie, and control your vining plant, it could turn into an arch rival instead of an arch wonder. Formal gardens and neat-and-tidy gardeners are much happier with hanging baskets and potted plants bedecking the entrance arch instead of an overenthusiastic vine.

HOW TALL TO BUILD AN ARCH

Part of the charm and intimacy of walking under an arch is that you know for a moment that the vastness of the outdoor sky has just been capped. No other garden feature gives you that same feeling of transition. For this reason, an outdoor arch can be built a bit lower than the doorway to a house, which is currently 6 feet 8 inches. One of the archways in our gardens is a mere 6 feet 2 inches, so that even average-sized visitors get the urge to duck as they pass through.

I admit we built this arch a little low on purpose for a personal reason: All 10 of my brothers and even my husband play basketball year-round. Basketball camps, basketball plays, and basketball teams are the subject of conversation at every family gathering. You might expect that the members of such a basketball-crazy family excel naturally at the sport because of their height. Unfortunately, just the opposite is true. Mother Nature did not cooperate with all the boyhood goals of the Callero boys, and although a few may be described as of average height, a majority of my brothers are short. Short and quick, short and spunky maybe, but never by the stretch of anyone's imagination would a brother of mine be considered tall. That is, until they visit my garden and feel like ducking to get under the archway. For just a few seconds, under that arch, even a 5-foot 6-inch point guard feels tall. Nobody has yet banged his or her head on our archway, but I have noticed a lot of smiles as the eyes gaze upward while someone is passing through it.

This story isn't meant to suggest that low archways should be constructed to boost the ego of short athletes. The seed I want to plant is that building your own garden structures gives you the freedom to break any design rules, size requirements, and stuffy building codes that you have to put up with when doing indoor construction. You can build paths wider than average or arches taller than needed, and you can make borders for your pathways in any style you want. This allows you to plan your structures to the scale of the garden. Short, narrow paths need lower archways; more substantial paths look better with higher, wider arches.

Pathways, borders, and arches define and outline your garden. Enjoy adding these flourishes, then stand back and admire the quick change in the appearance of your yard. You'll feel just like you did back in kindergarten, when you first learned to outline your coloring book pictures and realized how well borders worked to dress up your artwork, giving it that tidy, finished look.

SUREFIRE SHORTCUTS

❖ Cement curbing can be poured around your lawn by specialized curbing companies. They have equipment that can do the job without damaging the landscape. Check your phone directory.

❖ Use natural or unpainted wood for outdoor projects, and you won't have the added chore of painting.

❖ Sink all your lawn borders in at ground level so the mower can make a close cut, eliminating the need for edging.

❖ Make a screen of hanging plants for privacy on a patio or deck. In winter, when you aren't using the area, the plants will be gone, allowing for more sunlight to enter your home.

❖ A closet dowel and matching hardware is a quick way to add a rod for a hanging privacy garden. Position the dowel between the roof supports of a covered porch or patio.

❖ To economize and save time, install only three sections of your dream fence as a visual barrier. These sections can be used to screen off a front yard courtyard or to create a background for specimen plants.

❖ Dress up a boring fence line or blank wall by adding wall brackets for hanging plants. The metal brackets used for hanging closet shelves can also be used as hooks for hanging plants on walls or fences.

❖ Add charm to an established fence by adding wooden finials or fence post toppings. Birdhouses, carved animals, and other accents can also be displayed on fence posts.

❖ Dress up a boring gate with embellishments such as an archway added after the fact. Paint can be used to make the new and the old wood match.

Most-Asked Questions about Borders, Paths, and Arches

Q. *How do we get our neighbors to pay for half of the fence we would like to build? If we put in the labor, shouldn't they pay for more than half? Who gets to decide the color and style of the fence?*

A. If you're looking for a law that would force your neighbors to help pay for a fence, you can forget it. Paying for half of the fence materials that separates your yard from a neighbor's is a civilized tradition more popular in some parts of the country than others. The custom is that the party that builds the fence gets to decide on the style, but if your neighbor pays for half of the material, he or she is entitled to some say in the color and style of the fence. A so-called good-neighbor fence is when the slats or pickets are placed on alternate sides of the rails so that both parties see the finished side of the fence.

Q. *We are planting a laurel hedge around our backyard for privacy and wind control. One of our neighbors has told us we cannot plant within 3 feet of the property line, or the roots from our hedge will encroach on his lawn and rob moisture. How close to the property line should a hedge be planted, and how far apart should we space the plants?*

A. If you are planting an English laurel hedge *(Prunus laurocerasus)*, out of consideration to the neighbors, you should plant the hedge at least 6 feet from the property line. This broad-leaved evergreen shrub grows extremely fast and has greedy, far-reaching roots. You could control the root system by installing an underground barrier of metal stripping or poured cement to block the roots as they travel to the neighbor's yard.

Q. *How far apart and when do I plant small privet plants to get them to grow into a hedge?*

A. You can plant your hedge in early spring, midspring, early fall, or even winter if you live in a mild climate with only light frosts. A hedge planted in summer requires a lot of extra water and may be stressed by the heat. Privet plants (*Ligustrum* spp.) grow fast and can be spaced as close as 18 inches apart or as far as 30 inches apart, depending on how patient you are. If the plants you use are bare root (not in containers), you can dig a trench twice as wide as the root ball and lay the hedge plants in, adding the soil and standing the plants up as you go. If the plants are in containers, dig a hole for each plant but stagger the holes in a zigzag pattern, and the hedge will look filled in sooner.

Chapter Summary

- ❖ Adding borders to lawns and flowerbeds is a shortcut to a tidy garden and a finishing touch for any mature landscape.

- ❖ Garden walls in the form of fences, screens, and hedges can be improved to give the whole garden a more finished look.

- ❖ Bricks, landscape timbers, and rock borders are quick and inexpensive to install and can define the separate pocket gardens in your yard.

- ❖ Evergreen hedges can be dressed up with blooming plants positioned in front of them.

- ❖ Garden pathways and ornate fences can be built in stages using a four-step plan.

- ❖ Archways and arbors are low-maintenance shortcuts to a showcase garden. Arches act as dramatic entrances to garden rooms or separate the front yard from the back.

CHAPTER 7

The Finishing Touch

SHORTCUT:

*Add humor, whimsy,
and personality to
your landscape.*

The finishing touch, the icing on the cake, the final flourish for any garden should be a touch of whimsy. The little extras that make you smile or tell you about the owner's sense of humor are often referred to as whimsical accents — or the sign of an eccentric gardener. Senior-citizen gardeners are more likely to incorporate whimsical and personal touches, and when the creativity really gets going, these gardeners are classed as eccentrics. The question is, Do people need to grow old before becoming eccentric gardeners, or do eccentric gardeners know the secret of living well and just naturally live to a ripe old age?

For that matter, do large numbers of so-called eccentrics (in the context of original, imaginative, independent, nose-thumbers-at-society) take up gardening, or does spending many hours on your knees in the dirt create original, imaginative, and independent characters who don't mind waving their green thumbs at society?

This chapter on whimsy in the garden is written to encourage every home landscaper with her or his heart set on a showplace garden not to take the job too seriously. Throughout history, great landscape architects have designed spectacular gardens that have also bloomed with personality and showed budding good humor.

THE ART OF TOPIARY

Topiary, or the training and pruning of plant material into animal or other shapes, has been practiced for hundreds of years. Although high maintenance, it is also highly amusing. The best plant material for topiary works of whimsy are boxwood, yew, hemlock, and privet. An easy form to start with is to allow a rectangular hedge to grow humps by pruning only every other 3 feet off the top of the hedge. After one summer of growth, the high parts of the hedge can be trimmed into rounded forms, and the last hump can be turned into the head of a serpent or sea monster. An electric hedge trimmer makes quick work of topiary maintenance, but the more detailed the work is, the longer it takes for it to grow to maturity and the more difficult it is to maintain.

Wire-covered forms in the shape of teddy bears, ducks, and hearts are also used for whimsical topiary work. These forms are stuffed with sphagnum moss, and ivy is planted at the base. Potted ivy plants trained on a wire form are most often used indoors, but even an ivy ground cover can be trained to cover a sturdy wire form used out in the garden.

It was the French landscape designers in the 18th century who came up with the term *trompe l'oeil* (fool the eye) for latticework screens. These optical illusions were used on flat walls to give a garden more depth and play a joke on the viewer. Human-scale walk-through mazes were also popular all over Europe, with eye-blocking hedges of yew or holly creating walls of green that led puzzlers down blind alleys and into secret chambers.

But, it wasn't just the wealthy estate owners who added giggles to the garden. There are records of middle-class garden clubs suggesting to very proper Victorian ladies that they slyly plant maidenhair fern next to a stand of bachelor's button and, conceivably, a bit of baby's breath would pop up.

Even before all this Victorian fun and frolic, garden ha-has were constructed in England by the famous landscaper "Capability" Brown. A garden ha-ha was not a bad horticultural joke, but hedges or ditches created to hide a fence or boundary from view. Visitors to the garden vista could then borrow the background landscape of field and hill beyond and visually extend the scope of the garden view. The joke was on any visitor who naturally assumed that the grand stretch of land before her or him was one unbroken parcel rolling off into the distance. Something tells me that Mr. Brown, this gifted creator of ha-has and garden vistas, had quite a sense of humor to match his colorful nickname. This original thinker could be likened to a landscaping Robin Hood — one who robbed the great-looking views from the rich and made it look as though they belonged to the less rich.

The Greeks and Romans also realized that a garden was a place for laughing out loud, outrageously, and often. It was an ancient artist who first cast the mold for the classic fountain of a little boy relieving himself of something more than stress.

There are many other examples of fun and frolic in historic show gardens. Hedges pruned in the shape of leaping horses or running dogs, giant brass pigs, and tiny ceramic frogs are just a few of the show garden accents that are still putting smiles on the faces of visitors today.

Let these ideas inspire you to bring back the relaxed joy of being in a garden, or at least, to let loose and enjoy escaping outside as much as you did as a kid when the school bell rang. Don't get stuck thinking that the style of garden you most admire doesn't lend itself to a little levity. The whimsical garden ideas offered here are a few of the hundreds of ways you can add your personality and pizzazz to any style of garden.

Formal/Estate Style

Whimsical accents: Stone cherubs, odd flashes of color such as a single red geranium in a bed of white ones, lawn messages, mirrored gazing balls.

If any garden style needs a little lightening up, it's this one. Wooden tulips and pink flamingos are definitely out of place in the formal landscape, but that doesn't mean the design has to look as stiff and solemn as a bored butler's expression.

Choose subtle touches of joy and whimsy to contrast with the formal, symmetrical layout of an estate design. Consider one pink tulip in a rectangular bed of white ones, or a stone statue of a Greek goddess with red nail polish added to the toenails.

A garden lover traveling in Italy told me about a visit to a great Italian villa known for its formal landscape style. At the entrance to the villa was a collection of Greek statues done in the classic style of a young woman draped with folds of fabric. Down the road from this impressive display of wealth was the more humble home of a gardener with a small but formal front lawn. The entrance was shaded with olive trees and ornamented with the hilarious form of a naked store mannequin draped in an old sheet and standing proudly on a stone pedestal. The nude plastic mannequin may have been filling in the space on the empty pedestal until a real statue could be purchased, or perhaps she was meant to poke fun at the stiff formality of the nearby estate.

Using a mannequin in the garden is more of a prank than an outdoor accent, but it reminds us that we can enjoy the formality and symmetry of a classically designed garden and still add touches of humor mixed with irreverence — even if the only formal touch in your home landscape is that perfect patch of front lawn that too many of us waste time and money maintaining.

The velvety green lawn is a status symbol in many upscale neighborhoods, so it provides the perfect canvas for some friendly independence. A little creativity with a bag of fertilizer may be just the thing that will lighten the focus of the neighborhood lawn fanatics. Use a drop-style fertilizer spreader so you can control exactly where the fertilizer falls. A flour sifter might also work for a small area. Write your family name, address, or a cheery greeting with the granular fertilizer, and water carefully so as not to spread the granules. Only gradually will the neighbors realize that the deep green patches of grass in your lawn spell out words. Just think what you could do with stencils! Birthday greetings, anniversary wishes, or a generic welcome sign could be growing in

Grow a cheery greeting in your lawn.

your grass just a few days after your fertilizing rebellion. (See illustration.)

But enough of poking fun at classic garden designs. If you really want to add humor to the elegance and the tradition of a formal design, you need to choose beautiful props to show your lightheartedness. A stone angel perched on the ledge of a brick retaining wall and a cat sculpture crouched at the edge of a fountain are more conservative examples of garden accents that add a whimsical flourish to a formal garden.

There is another classic shape that visually delights any observer of a formal/estate garden. This is an accent that could never roll from the boundaries of impeccably good taste. I'm suggesting the addition of a perfect sphere chiseled from granite or a similar stone. These stone spheres come in a range of sizes and were originally used to top entrance pillars at gatehouses. The look of a sphere centered on top of a rectangular column is truly a classic exercise in architecture. But times have changed and so have ways to use that stone ball. Display the orb imaginatively, setting it, for contrast, amid wispy or spiky ornamental grasses. Or display a trio of balls in a corner of a patio. Use

Whimsy can even be used in a formal garden.

the clean lines and globular shape anywhere an unusual outdoor accent is needed, even if it's in the middle of a lawn.

I'm getting irreverent about the classical again, but I just can't forget a photograph I once saw. The stone sphere was sitting on a patch of grass in a formal garden with roses and herb beds nearby. The scene-stealing item was a pair of plastic hands coming up out of the lawn as if reaching to grab the stone ball. It was a remarkable piece of outdoor art, and an idea that would be fun to imitate in your backyard — or even the front yard, if your neighbors have a great sense of humor about unusual adornments.

You can have your formal garden and a bit of whimsy, too. You just need to be more subtle with your touches of humor.

Country/Cottage Style

Whimsical accents: Whirligigs; folk art; wooden lawn signs; wooden tulips stuck into window boxes; gates made from wheels; brightly painted shutters, doors, and window frames; decorated birdhouses.

Drive down a country lane on a windy day, and you may see a farmer milking his cow, arms pumping up and down rhythmically, or a logger sawing at a stump that never seems to diminish. These toy-size action figures are called whirligigs. They're wooden, wind-powered, painted figures mounted on a pole or fence with a small propeller attached to catch the breeze. Whirligigs bring movement, rhythm, and a delightful sense of fun to the country garden.

Cottage gardeners of the past and present indulge themselves with other lively accents as well. Metal birdcages filled with hanging flowers and brightly plumed plastic parrots swinging from tree branches can be found in English cottage gardens even today. Colorful accents like these can be so downright tacky that they're endearing. Plastic flowers are also being used in some cottage-style gardens, in England, but this is where I draw the line.

Lawn signs that warn of "attack cats", and wooden cutouts of a lady's posterior caught in the bend-over position with bloomers showing are other examples of corny-but-classic lawn ornaments. Other ideas to consider for your country garden are wooden tulips stuck in window boxes and planters or a trompe l'oeil mural of farm animals or painted pets on a garden shed.

Looking through a travel book promoting driving of country roads, I was enchanted by a realistic mural done on a weathered garden shed. Old tools, sacks of feed, and piles of clay pots were depicted with such accuracy that I thought I was actually viewing the inside of the shed. Painted in the corner was a gray cat curled up for a nap.

I must have been thinking of this scene when I took a shortcut to decorating an outdoor wall with garden tools myself. This landscape-decorating project was done on camera for a local television show. We were trying to promote Goodwill Industries as a place where gardeners can go to find recycled pots, tools, and outdoor furniture. In an effort to inspire urban renewal of outdoor spaces, we did a before-and-after segment using a courtyard located at the Seattle, Washington, warehouse. Keep in mind that we had only a few hours, a few plants, and a few cans of spray paint to transform the outdoor space into something visually pleasing. Of course, we could also use any of the recycled tools that had been donated to Goodwill.

This is where that painted shed comes back into the story. I don't have the talent to do a painting of a tool on a wall, but I certainly was able to paint a tool and hang it on the wall as a piece of outdoor art. The blank wooden wall that hemmed in the courtyard became a canvas for red, yellow, and green tools displayed in a random pattern. We took rusty rakes, shovels, and trowels, sprayed them with rust-resistant outdoor paint (the kind made for metal lawn furniture), and used bent nails to fasten them to the once-boring but now brightly punctuated wall. The idea did not look as bizarre as it sounds once we painted pots, a metal table, and a bench in the same bright colors and added blooming primroses and hanging ivy to the once-dismal scene.

The magic of television showed how the transformation took place step by step, and I was so proud of this off-the-wall decor that I expected to see brightly painted tools nailed to the sides of sheds and garages as soon as the show aired. Oddly enough, no one seems to have followed my lead, and the streets of Seattle are still safe from spray-painted castoffs disguised as works of art.

Other displays of country humor are more likely to be found in open spaces than in urban places. For instance, I couldn't help but smile when I drove past a pair of wooden, fleece-covered sheep forms grazing contentedly in a fenced front yard.

If you love the cozy and simple look of country-style decorating, add that down-home feeling to the exterior of your home with imaginative planters, simple folk art porch ornaments, and the whimsical touches of whirligigs, lawn signs, and homemade treasures. Country accents are available at craft fairs and gift shops, but most are painted for indoor use. You can prime your country treasures for outdoor display by spraying the painted surfaces with shellac or a clear plastic coating. Display the art under the cover of a porch or roof overhang, and store it indoors during the winter months to protect the painted finish.

As proof that these ornaments can last for many years, I offer the wooden cutout of a large goose that I received as a housewarming gift 7 years ago. This country goose wears a red bandanna and a smile as she waddles through the vegetable garden (never going anyplace because she's anchored by a stake in the ground). The cotton bandanna faded away after just one summer in the elements, and the stake used to anchor the goose rotted in the moist soil of our raised beds after just 2 years. The painted face and body of the whimsical goose are still in fine shape, however, and this garden accent is put to good use helping to prop up tomato plants and doing duty as a scarecrow as she is rotated about the vegetable beds. I've even laid the goose on top of a freshly planted seedbed for a day or two, to discourage our cats from digging in the soft soil. Even whimsical accents can have some purely practical applications.

Contemporary/Oriental Style

Whimsical accents: Symbolic rivers of rock, thyme, or moss; stone fish; Oriental writing on large boulders; drifts of color from minor bulbs.

The peaceful and serene mood that is part of a Japanese-influenced landscape can be improved by a cheerful interruption of garden whimsy. Think of using joyful touches of color next to a dry streambed in the form of tiny bulbs blooming on the banks. The snowdrop *(Galanthus nivalis)* and dwarf daffodil *(Narcissus minimus)* are two examples of miniature flowers that can bring subtle color to a purposely subdued garden.

The image of running water in an Oriental garden is so important that one of the most effective shortcuts is to add the illusion of a streambed by using gravel and rock. A streambed illusion can also become a setting for your more creative touches of imagination. In my own garden, I planted a sea-green carpet of woolly thyme in a long, curving shape to imitate a river. The rocks alongside this bed are smooth boulders, so there is no question that this is a river of thyme. A few companion plants add to the river look. Sea pink *(Armeria)* is a grassy perennial with globular pink blooms that should be grown near every dry streambed just because of its wonderful scene-setting name. The tall, flat foliage of the iris family is also found growing near water, so I used several types of irises near our river of thyme to add to the waterfront feeling. Adding a bridge or boardwalk on piers over your artificial waterway is another way to play up the illusion of water. Irish or Scotch moss *(Sagina subulata)* or any other low-growing ground cover can be used in place of thyme to form the riverbed.

The vision of an actual bridge over an imitation stream reminds me of the wonderful Japanese garden exhibit displayed one year at an indoor flower and garden show. The Oriental moon gate and ornate tea house used in this display garden were impressive but difficult to duplicate in a home garden. But, there was a small whimsical touch that had many visitors pointing fingers and smiling. Set amid the large boulders and fine gravel of a dry streambed was a pair of stone fish heads. Carved from rock to blend in with the gravel river, they looked just like a pair of slightly smiling salmon caught in the act of gulping air as they swam upstream to spawn. If fish carved from stone are not to your liking, consider a stone-colored frog or turtle as an accent for your waterless streambed.

Rocks and boulders are very important in Japanese gardens, and many people realize that their placement in the garden has deep symbolism. The large rocks in our own Japanese-style garden area are heavy with symbolism — and a symbol of their own heaviness — because they were just too large to move when we started to put in a lawn. We built a garden using the boulders as a focal point instead. You can add to the giant rocks in your own Japanese design by painting the Japanese symbols for happiness, laughter, or love on your boulder signpost. The strokes of paint in Japanese-style script can also be used to decorate a fence, garden wall, or bamboo mat hung near the front door.

In your own garden, you don't have to follow any set of rules. Adopt a garden style to influence your design, but never let that influence become restrictive. Japanese gardens are designed to bring peace and contentment into the lives of the viewer. You can borrow inspiration from authentic Oriental gardens and still be true to the purpose for which these gardens are built without getting caught up in its rules and regulations. If you want to grow old-fashioned roses or blooming perennials in your contemporary/Oriental-style garden but fear that they will look out of place, go ahead and try it anyway. Many gardens that start out in a certain style evolve into something quite different as the tastes and interests of the gardener grow along with the garden itself.

If you decide you want to keep the authentic look of a Japanese garden, any touches of humor or whimsy must be extremely subtle. However, if your garden style is more contemporary than Oriental, you can loosen those chains of conformity and display modern sculptures, unusual plant shapes, and inventive recycled materials in your landscape. Uncluttered openness and clean lines are preferred in contemporary architecture and landscape designs, and nontraditional accents work well in these open spaces. In a contemporary-style landscape, your imagination and sense of fun can be as unrestricted as modern art.

Naturalistic/Woodland Style

Whimsical accents: Forest animals, furniture made from twigs or stumps, wood carvings, carved wooden poles.

This garden style is easy to infuse with a little fantasy, as wood nymphs, forest animals and stump carvings look quite at home. The rustic quality of this type of garden means many of the lighthearted accents are simple for the homeowner to make.

Woodland gardeners lucky enough to have stumps on the property have a source of much inspiration. Large stumps can be carved with a chain saw to make earthy benches for outdoor seating. Champion chain saw artists can do remarkable carvings of bears, eagles, and other creatures to turn fallen logs and stumps into rustic outdoor sculptures. In our part of the country, logging employs thousands of woodworkers, so driving past a garden with a life-sized grizzly bear carved from a former cedar tree or seeing a newly cut tree laid on its side and being turned into a totem pole is not unusual. One family had a cedar tree removed but left the stump protruding 6 feet into the air. They had a chain saw artist chisel a pair of bear cubs into the stump, and suddenly, the view from their family room window had year-round charm, and the tree that once cloaked the patio in darkness now lightens the backyard with levity. Another homeowner used an apple-and-leaf stencil (and her imagination) to transform a no-longer-used drainpipe on the garden wall into a fantasy tree with ever-fresh fruit.

Stencil a garden motif on a wall.

If you live far from a community of wood carvers and still like a woodsy, natural feeling in your landscape you can add other outdoor accents to give your garden the look of an enchanted forest. Use pliable plastic strips to make a homemade form, and pour stepping-stones in the shape of a giant's footstep. It will look as though Sasquatch has left his mark.

Backyards left natural for kids to play in can be enhanced with a playhouse that looks like the candy cottage from Hansel and Gretel or the home of Goldilocks and the Three Bears. Log cabins, wooden bridges, and fence lines and screens made from rope and poles are other imaginative ways to show your lighter side. I even visited a charming woodland garden that used a pile of rocks left by the previous owner. Rather than pay to have the rocks removed, the new owners built a rocky cavelike grotto and encouraged moss to cover the surface. Too small for a person to enter, this little shelter contained a miniature table-and-chair set that suggested a troll of some kind was about to return home.

Twig furniture and Adirondack chairs are two types of garden seating befitting a woodland garden. Wood that is coated with a preservative but left unpainted blends in with the forest feeling in a natural garden. If bark and branches are left on these outdoor pieces, the texture adds even more of a rustic accent. Add an amusing object used as a planter, such as an old metal watering can or hollowed-out log, and you have a whimsical focal point that doesn't deviate from the natural woodland setting.

Sitting next to a rustic bench right outside my bedroom window is an old pair of leather work boots that a grandparent once wore. The boots have a hole cut out of each toe, and from this opening and the top of the boots grow shallow-rooted succulents. This pair of leather planters makes a rustic garden accent and is meant to remind me of that old gardener's adage: The best fertilizers for any garden are the footsteps of the owner.

Mediterranean/Desert Style

Whimsical accents: Painted pottery, bleached driftwood, colorful tile, stone lizards, Texas-style accents such as cowboy hats and lariats displayed on a wall.

The sun-drenched climates of the Mediterranean and southwestern United States are natural environments for the casual, outdoor living that this style of landscaping encourages. It is easy to add a touch of personality and whimsy with pieces of painted pottery and unusual cacti. Succulents and cacti can grow in very little soil, so a pair of cowboy boots nailed to a wall and a hat sitting on a bench can be used as whimsical plant containers.

Wrought-iron and metal accents blend well with any Spanish-inspired garden. Recycled metal castoffs, such as the curved pieces of iron from the headboard of a bed, can become a whimsical (and doubly ironic) flowerbed. Outdoor seating can be fun and creative, as well as unconventional. Consider using very bright and intense colors on your sunny patio. One of the quickest shortcuts to a new look is a fresh coat of paint on the old patio furniture. To go from pretty to whimsical, choose a vibrant color such as turquoise or red instead of the traditional black, white, or pastel. Remember that paint for metal outdoor furniture comes in easy-to-use spray cans. You don't even have to limit yourself to one color of paint on the furniture. Paint each slat on your old wooden benches a different primary color, or paint each leg of your wrought-iron table a different pastel color. Use an inexpensive plastic tablecloth with all the colors in it to draw together the rainbow of colors. Not only is working with paint quick and inexpensive, but if your wild ideas get out of control, mistakes are easy to cover up.

Patios are an important part of outdoor living, and if you need to replace broken tiles, consider adding extra life to the design by replacing them with random pieces of art tiles engraved with animal shapes or handprints. You can also use tile in a spiral pattern similar to the start of the Yellow Brick Road in the land of Oz.

Stucco and cement walls are often used to border courtyards in Mediterranean/desert-style gardens, and these walls can be a display area for outdoor art. Going beyond the typical red clay sun or bright tile plaque that usually adorns these walls, one do-it-yourselfer took several ceramic teacups and set them into the face of his newly constructed wall before the cement dried. Only half of the cup protrudes from the wall, giving the flat surface interesting shadows, and the bowls of the cups are just large enough to use as outdoor vases, making these lighthearted accents useful as well.

In a garden with a sunny climate, you can grow low, compact succulents such as hen and chickens or miniature cacti. Add whimsy to the planting pattern by arranging plants in blocks so that the garden bed looks like a checkerboard. Growers of succulents or low ground covers can remove a few bricks from a patio and use the space as an unexpected spot to plant for close-up color, replacing the traditional container gardens on the patio. Sweet alyssum is a reseeding annual that prospers when grown in cracks or the gaps left by missing bricks. This idea is a great excuse for never getting around to resurfacing or repairing a damaged patio.

Create a whimsical "flowerbed".

SUREFIRE SHORTCUTS

❖ Rotate your garden accents so they always bring unexpected pleasure.

❖ Use a can of spray paint in a lively color to brighten old metal tools and hang them on the side of a garden shed or garage for instant outdoor art.

❖ A reverse of the idea above is to make stencils in the shapes of your tools, tape them to the wall, and spray-paint the entire building. Remove the stencils to reveal the tool outlines, and you may even find yourself hanging your tools up in their proper shadows for tidy storage.

❖ Use the base of an old stump to display a miniature table-and-chair set or a doll-sized watering can and tiny clay pots. Spray everything with waterproof shellac to protect it from the weather, and use wood glue to keep the pieces in place.

❖ Nail a pair of leather boots or bright plastic rain boots on a tree or porch and plant in them.

❖ Dress up the vegetable garden with a white picket fence or rustic split-rail fence and stick a metal mailbox on a post right in the middle. Paint the mailbox or use it plain as a convenient and protected place to store your seeds, gloves, and trowel. Use colorful wooden row markers painted with pictures of corn, peas, tomatoes, and so on, to brighten up the early-spring garden and remind you to get those seeds planted.

❖ Purchase colorful yards of waterproof oilcloth from a fabric store. Cut squares to wrap around your faded outdoor furniture cushions, much like using slipcovers on upholstered furniture. Use leftover scraps to wrap around flowerpots and make table covers.

❖ Outline a garden bed with bricks or rocks in the shape of a cat's head. Form a large circle with two triangles on top for ears. Plant the bed with different varieties of catnip.

❖ If you have trouble getting the guests to come to the right door, stencil footprints or arrows onto the pathway, using outdoor surface paint sold for making lines on basketball and tennis courts.

(Continued on p. 158)

❖ One of the most practical and whimsical signs to use in your garden has only two words: Smell me. Move this marker about as the seasons change and different fragrant flowers come into bloom.

❖ Insulated metal milk boxes, the type that are metal outside and Styrofoam inside, make practical porch containers for growing geraniums and other half-hardy annuals. The insulated nature of these boxes allows petunias, geraniums, and other marginally hardy annuals to survive a freezing winter.

These examples and suggestions should encourage you to break the rules and get creative with your home landscape. Choosing a garden style, using traditional plant groupings, and following a plan are all good ideas, but not the only ways to create a wonderful garden. Never let the worry of deviating from the norm or breaking design rules rob you of the joy of gardening. Gardens are grown for beauty and personal pleasure, and gardeners must remember to enjoy themselves as they beautify the world.

Most-Asked Questions about Finishing Touches

Q. *I am not a handy do-it-yourself artist. Where do you suggest that buy-it-yourself collectors like me find unusual outdoor accents?*

A. Your quest for whimsical accents can take you to import shops where pottery, baskets, ironwork, and outdoor furniture abound, or to art and craft fairs where artists sell whirligigs and other outdoor handicrafts. There are several mail-order catalog companies that specialize in garden accents. If you really want something original, consider commissioning a local artist or craftsperson to design tiles, outdoor furniture, or a collection of pottery.

Q. *How do I tell my neighbors that their plastic geese and raccoons are tacky and that their yard has too many garden ornaments?*

A. It seems to me you have more of a problem than your neighbor does. Let them adorn their property as they want, and you decorate your garden the way you prefer. Learn to enjoy the sense of fun and frolic that your neighbors are so generously sharing with the world. And, be thankful those aren't real geese in his front yard — large fowl can be very noisy.

Chapter Summary

❖ An imaginative use of fun and whimsy has been a part of garden design throughout history. Take a shortcut to a more creative garden by adding a little irreverence, a surprise accent, or a creative planting plan to your landscape — just for the fun of it.

❖ The more formal and subdued look of the estate and contemporary/Oriental garden styles are best enhanced with subtle touches of whimsy. Country-style gardens can handle the less-inhibited accents of folk art and yard signs, whereas naturalistic/woodland gardens can pull off enchanting accents with more of a storybook style. The Mediterranean/desert garden style is best able to handle the intensity of bright and unusual color; contemporary landscapes can be canvases for unusual and irreverent outdoor sculptures.

CHAPTER 8

Whirlwind Weekends and 48-Hour Fix-Ups

Now that you've read about the seven shortcuts to a showier landscape, it's time to use them as a road map for improving some typical home landscapes. These major make-overs are broken down into smaller projects that can be accomplished in 48 hours or during a whirlwind of work over a productive weekend. The reality is that most homeowners take months or even years to improve their landscapes, working on and off over many weekends.

A warning label should be affixed to all the before-and-after transformations: These projects can be accomplished in a weekend, but not *all* of them can be done in the same weekend. Pace yourself, spread out the projects over a reasonable period of time, and try to complete one improvement before moving on to the next. Most people enjoy starting things more than finishing them. (Consider the number of people who have bolts of fabric stored but never sewn, expensive woodworking tools collecting dust, and exercise equipment worth thousands of dollars being used as clothes hangers.) Breaking down these make-overs into small projects should help you discipline yourself to finish them. Try to use the start of a new project as a reward for finishing an earlier one. When in doubt about where to begin, remember the advice from Chapter 1 about starting close to the front door and working your way out toward the edges of the property, adding plants, paths, and borders as you go.

The Make-Over Candidates

The front yards receiving the make-overs here are composites of many landscapes I have helped design over the years. They represent the most common problems and design preferences of real homeowners. When I ask a new homeowner her or his most important consideration in planning a new landscape, I can usually count on one of four (and sometimes all four) answers:

1. "We want to save money" (the budget-conscious make-over).

2. "We want to have less work" (the low-maintenance make-over).

3. "We want to use less water" (the drought-tolerant make-over).

4. "We want it to look natural and to attract wildlife" (the native plant make-over).

All homeowners want the results to be immediate. Even dedicated garden lovers prefer shortcuts and instant gratification, because once the big decisions have been made and a master plan is in place, they'll have years of puttering and rearranging to do, and plenty of time for the real heart of gardening — improving the soil and becoming intimately familiar with plants. The four make-overs presented in this chapter represent very different garden styles and client priorities. What they all have in common is how they use the seven shortcuts presented in the preceding chapters.

Make-Over 1: A Budget-Conscious Country/Cottage Landscape

"How much is this going to cost me?" is the first question many homeowners ask, and for good reason. Borrowing to their limit just to get into their first house, many homeowners will be paying for all the landscaping out of their regular monthly budget instead of taking out a loan or dipping into a large savings account. These homeowners are also likely to do all the planting and installation themselves, and they are likely to be virgin gardeners — those who have never owned a yard and don't realize that caring for a bed of roses (and a lawn, a perennial garden, and shrubs) isn't always a bed of roses. Maintaining even a small yard to show garden standards takes considerable skill, so if the owners are virgin gardeners on a budget, I avoid suggesting the more demanding perennial plants that need staking, improved soil, or winter protection.

You may notice that the plants used in this design are easier to grow and more readily available at nurseries than those in the other landscape designs. The very practical reason for this is that the most common and easiest-topropagate species of trees and shrubs are usually the least expensive. (In the Pacific Northwest, that means juniper tams, rhododendrons, and azaleas in gallon pots.) Many new homeowners confess that they buy most of their plants from discount stores, watching the ads until they see the "3-for-$10" specials that discount stores use as loss leaders and display in makeshift parking-lot nurseries.

I try to encourage every home landscaper to plant a few of the less commonly used shrubs and trees that only a full-service nursery carries, just to give some variety to the neighborhood landscape. The truth is that even though more experienced gardeners are anxious to explore nurseries and plant catalogs for interesting plant varieties, the budget-conscious or virgin gardener may not have the interest, experience, time, or money to hunt for spectacular specimen plants or unusual ground covers and perennials. This make-over is sensitive to that fact.

Recycled Plant Material

Another point needs to be considered when planning a landscape for the new homeowner on a budget. These people often are the recipients of gift plants, orphaned plants, overgrown plants, and recycled plants from friends and relatives. Entire yards have been beautifully landscaped from other people's cast-off, overgrown plants, and donations of ground covers, perennial divisions, and cuttings. Instead of disregarding these hand-me-downs and dig-me-ups, I suggest that new homeowners announce that they are in the market for plant adoptions. An unusual and unrelated collection of misshapen plant material may be offered, but you can usually depend on at least some of the donated plants being healthy, well adapted to the climate, and easy to grow. Why else would these plants be given away, unless they were successful at reproducing or enlarging?

My only warnings are to reject diseased or bug-infested donations and large trees and shrubs with deep root systems that are unlikely to survive a transplant. My other advice is to designate an area of the yard to warehouse the newcomers until a decision can be made about to where to plant them. It helps if this storage area is called the friendship garden. Plants that friends bring to share can be quickly and temporarily planted there until their true personalities can be determined and a suitable growing location chosen.

The shady side of a house or shed is a good place to establish a friendship garden. Most plants arrive freshly dug and slightly stressed from the uprooting ordeal, and a cool, shady spot protected from the wind buys time until you can decide whether the newcomers are worthy of permanent adoption into your landscape or are merely visiting troublemakers. Among the latter are ground covers and vines that take up too much room; shrubs whose buds suffer constant winter blasts and never bloom; flowering plants that need constant staking, feeding, or pleading to keep them looking decent; and plants you simply don't like and won't use — even if they are free.

I should confess that my own friendship garden is full of perennial plants that I should get rid of. Either they grow too tall and spindly for our shady property, or they attract slugs from miles around and sport lacy-looking foliage. There are many reasons that some of those plants should be made into compost or given away, but I just can't bring myself to dig them up. Some have sentimental value, given to me by generous fellow gardeners, and some I'm hoping are ugly ducklings that will eventually grow into beautiful plants. Hope springs eternal, and each year I wait for spring and eternally hope that the ugly ducklings will be transformed into swans with the change of seasons. There's never yet been such a winter transformation, but each year, as I consider tossing out the misfits, I rationalize that I'm not the perfect gardener, so how can I demand perfection from my plants? My friendship garden remains a ragtag collection of unrelated plants not handsome enough to work into the main part of the landscape but too healthy to dig and dump.

Shortcut 1: Get Organized

The first thing to do is to look at the house, consider your personal tastes, and choose a landscaping style that fits. For example, an L-shaped rambler has no definite style, but its simple front door and peaked roofline make it a good candidate for a cottage garden. This means that embellishments such as shutters, window boxes, latticework, and picket fences can add to the cottage atmosphere. Roses, flowering vines, tall perennials, and blooming trees are the types of plants used in traditional cottage gardens, but that doesn't mean that all of these plants have to be used in this landscape. An island of lawn can be included, along with simple, country-style garden accents.

❖ Sketch or walk the property, planning for the location of the trees and shrub boundaries and the size of the center lawn.

❖ Decide on the location of a focal point, whether pathways need to be added or widened, and the location of practical items such as garbage cans, a dog kennel, or a clothesline.

- ❖ Remember to plan for a friendship garden or storage area screened from view so that the landscape will look neat and tidy as the transformation process is taking place.

- ❖ Planning is a good project to take on in the winter because so much of it involves browsing through catalogs and magazines and deciding on blooming plants and the style of fence, bench, and plant containers you can afford.

Shortcut 2: Improve the Front Entry

- ❖ Paint, pots, and a front yard sitting area can turn even a simple cement stoop in front of a modest rambler into a front entry garden.

- ❖ Start with the front door. Sweep away the cobwebs and cut back any overgrown shrubbery.

- ❖ Paint the front door a different, darker color than the color used for the house. Add shutters to the windows and matching shutters down the sides of the door if there is room. Don't paint the shutters the same color as the house. To save money, buy narrow, unfinished shutters from a home center and paint them yourself with a weather-protective finish.

- ❖ Hang a seasonal door wreath, straw hat, or moss basket from the door or near the porch to lend the doorway a cottage atmosphere. A hanging half-basket can also be attached to the wall. Four-inch

---

USING RECYCLED BRICK

Bricks salvaged from old chimneys or construction can be used in landscaping projects. To solve the problem of not having enough bricks for the job, mix new and used-looking bricks with the salvaged bricks. You can even mix three or four different styles from many small salvage jobs for a rustic country look. To clean dry mortar and cement from old bricks, soak them for a few hours, then use a hammer and chisel to chip off the debris.

---

pots of pansies or other flowers can be slipped into this basket and rotated with seasonal flowering plants and evergreen boughs for continuous color.

❖ Clear out any plants near a narrow walkway or in the crook of an L-shaped path. Use this corner as a gravel-covered courtyard. Bricks can be used for this area if you can scrounge some recycled ones at a bargain price. Opening up this area makes the path to the front door seem wider and more spacious, gives you a pleasant place to sit, and provides a stage to display container gardens and folk art.

Shortcut 3: Create a Vista

❖ Add stepping-stones in front of flowerbeds below the front windows to lead the eye toward a lattice archway on the side of the house. The lawn can also serve as a clearing so that from inside the house there is a direct view of a focal point tree. The same type of surface used to make the front yard courtyard can be used to form the pathway that leads to this arch. If gravel is used, stepping-stones should also be added if the pathway is going to get much foot traffic, as loose gravel is difficult to walk on.

❖ Plant a matching set of low shrubs across the front of the yard to lead the eye toward a focal point.

❖ Install the posts now for a picket fence behind the low shrubs. You may damage the roots if you dig next to these shrubs later on.

Shortcut 4: Use Nonliving Focal Points

❖ Add a country or park-style bench to the front courtyard to draw the eye toward this area. Set stepping-stones in the gravel for the legs of the bench to rest on if the ground is not quite level. Even a simple backless bench like the type used with picnic tables works as a focal point. Use paint and stencils to dress up a simple bench and turn it into a charming country feature.

❖ Add a lattice arch or a simpler arch to the side of the house. Prebuilt lattice archways are often available at home center stores.

❖ Add the birdbath to the clearing in the rose garden, or substitute a sundial sitting on a cement-pipe pedestal, a birdhouse on a post, or even a fan-shaped trellis supporting a climbing rose.

Shortcut 5: Spotlight Show-off Plants

❖ Choose a tree to use in the corner of the landscape, but elevate the area by mounding the soil so that the tree sits higher than the lawn. The tree is also framed with space because no other tall plants are allowed to grow nearby. A flowering plum is a good choice for a show-off tree because it can usually be purchased bare root in early spring for less money than an evergreen or a potted flowering tree. The plants used at the base of the tree could be primroses and crocuses because these flowers bloom early, at the same time as the plum. Once spring has sprung, these flowers will fade and the pink blossoms of the plum tree will be replaced with burgundy leaves. This is when the gray foliage of dusty miller can be added to the mound around the tree. Dusty miller and small bulbs are both easy to find and inexpensive, making them good choices for beginning gardeners on a budget.

❖ Plant roses in a side rose garden and position this pocket garden next to the driveway for the following reasons: It's more convenient to admire and cut the roses without walking across a damp lawn, and it's more convenient for daily checks of the plants for insects and disease.

A rose garden is not very attractive in winter and early spring, so a location right in front of the house could be distracting during those months. Rose plants are great bargains for penny-pinching gardeners because a single plant blooms all summer the first year, and with proper protection will bloom again and again in future years. Old-fashioned roses and the new shrub roses are good choices because their more casual growth forms and open flowers personify the cottage garden look, and their hardier, more disease-resistant nature makes them less likely to require pesticides and specific pruning practices.

Shortcut 6: Outline the Boundaries

❖ Add cross-rails and pickets to the fence posts across the front of the yard. This fence is appropriate for a budget-conscious make-over because only three sections of fencing are used.

❖ Plant recycled shrubs to make a green wall along the sides of the property, or purchase young shrubs and allow them to grow into a living hedge.

❖ Use landscape timbers or recycled bricks to border the gravel paths and lawn area.

❖ Add a trellis screen or simple arbor behind the rose garden to form another wall and act as a support for rambling roses or an overhead vine.

❖ Frame the archway on the side of the house with a pair of evergreen shrubs to make a green wall between the front yard and back.

❖ The L-shaped configuration of the house forms walls on two sides of the courtyard garden. Use these walls for hanging baskets and folk art displays.

Shortcut 7: Add a Whimsical Accent

Many country/cottage-style accents work with this style of landscape, but for a limited budget, choose recycled materials.

❖ Use a recycled wooden planter and renew it with a fresh coat of paint to match the bench or trim used in the front entry.

❖ Visit tag sales and thrift shops for unusual country objects to use as containers or outdoor accents.

❖ Lay an old whiskey barrel or bucket on its side and plant low-growing flowers or a ground cover in it so that it looks as though the plants are spilling out from the overturned bucket.

MISTAKES TO AVOID FOR A SMALL YARD ON A BUDGET

❖ Don't place a tall fence or high screening across the front of a tiny yard.

❖ Keep the arch used on the side of the house in scale with the roofline. A single-story house is dwarfed by an archway as tall as the roof overhang.

❖ If you invest a lot of money in nonliving focal points, make sure they are the type you can take with you if you move to a larger home. Birdbaths, sundials, and pottery can be used in future gardens, but fences, arches, and trees must stay when you sell the house. The average American moves every 7 years.

❖ If there is only to be one small tree in the front yard, invest in one that is deserving of all the attention it will get. This is not the place to plant a misshapen hand-me-down or a recycled shrub that outgrew its welcome in someone else's yard.

❖ The trim color on the door, windows, and shutters can be the same, but paint the front fence sections white or a neutral color. Matching the color of the fence to the doorway garden makes the entire yard seem smaller because it draws the fence visually closer to the house.

❖ If you're a virgin gardener, don't pay for unusual perennials or expensive blooming or rare shrubs until you have a chance to improve the soil and learn what permanent plants will look like year-round. Use annual flowers or bedding plants to fill up the space the first year or two until you learn more about gardening and your own plant preferences.

❖ One of the best bargains for a small yard is to live next to someone with a lovely landscape. Don't try to close in your landscape by installing garden walls along the property line when you can enjoy the beautiful scenery right next door or across the street.

Make-Over 2: A Low-Maintenance Formal/Estate Landscape

The homeowners in this make-over want a formal/estate look with low maintenance. They plan to hire a lawn care company to maintain the grass and to putter a bit with the flowerbeds, but because they are retired, travel a lot, or have demanding careers, they have no interest in cultivating a lot of plants. This collection of shortcuts works well in a neighborhood of traditional formal homes, especially if the lots are small.

Shortcut 1: Get Organized

There is a two-story brick archway and brick trim across the front of the house, and traditional architecture demands that this landscape style be formal, tidy, and traditional. No sprawling shrubs and wildflower displays for this front yard! The plants used in a low-maintenance, formal design should be compact, dense, and upright.

❖ Map out the size and shape of the front lawn, keeping in mind that a simple oval or rectangular shape is the most formal and easiest to care for.

❖ Get bids on projects to lower future maintenance, such as a raised brick planter to echo the shape of a bay window.

❖ Plot out the shape of the walkways, making them as wide as possible to eliminate maintenance.

Shortcut 2: Improve the Front Entry

❖ In this make-over, two large cement urns were placed on the entry porch. The footed base makes them more formal and impressive than traditional clay pots or wooden planters. The urns are used as decorative holders for 6-inch pots of plants purchased full-grown and in bloom. Examples of formal-looking plants sold in 6-inch pots are tulips in spring, geraniums in summer, mums in fall, and holly sprigs in winter. When the seasons change, these plants are lifted out of the urns, pot and all, and replaced with a seasonal plant.

❖ A mulch of wood chips covers the rim of the plastic pots, and gravel fills the bottom of these urns. The gravel base keeps the potted plants from sitting in their own drainage water.

❖ There are two planting areas on either side of the porch, but these areas are under the roof overhang, and any plant grown here requires watering by hand. Fill these spaces with gravel up to the same level as the cement porch. Then add a formal iron or stone bench to the new gravel surface.

❖ Add shiny brass kickplates and decorative knobs to double doors. Also, add a large hanging light fixture to draw attention to a high roof over the porch.

❖ Add a wrought-iron railing to the sides of the steps and around the flowerbed near the front path. Wrought iron is used as an accent in other parts of the garden as well because it is formal, low maintenance, and quick to install.

Shortcut 3: Create a Vista

❖ Add a pathway off of the side of the house to draw attention to a garden gate.

❖ An evergreen hedge along the side of a path helps to frame the formal scene.

❖ Plant the formal flowerbed alongside the driveway with a ribbon of color. If a line of white flowers is used to lead the eye, white flowers are also planted at the base. A lower-maintenance option is to use a ribbon of white rocks.

Shortcut 4: Use Nonliving Focal Points

Nonliving focal points are used extensively in this low-maintenance make-over. A wrought-iron gate, brick lampposts, and a sculpture garden are used as substitutes for flowering trees and other specimen plants.

❖ Have brick lampposts installed at the start of the driveway. This project may be too difficult for an inexperienced do-it-yourselfer, but it takes the place of trees and shrubs in this area. Use rocks or mulch at the base of the pillars; grass would be difficult to mow around here.

- Lay a pad for outdoor artwork in the sculpture garden using flagstones, bricks, or cement pavers as a floor.

- Find an appropriate piece of traditional garden artwork to use as a focal point in the newly paved area. A weather globe, a classic sundial, a bench, or a fountain work well.

Shortcut 5: Spotlight Show-Off Plants

This low-maintenance landscape will have very few specimen plants to show off. A grafted Japanese maple that can be seen from inside and outside and flowerbeds near the front walkway are the places to add seasonal color.

- Plant a dwarf evergreen or weeping Japanese maple. Bulbs and bedding plants can be used to give seasonal color. A raised planter is easy to work in without a lot of bending and kneeling.

- Use a low, spreading evergreen such as Scotch moss in the flowerbed or a mass planting of bedding plants. Be sure to choose low-maintenance flowers that don't need a lot of pinching and pruning to keep them looking neat and formal. Geraniums are a good choice if the area is sunny; fibrous begonias and impatiens work well if the bed is shaded from the hot afternoon sun. In spring, use tulips to fill this bed. In winter, a fresh mulch of wood chips will keep it looking neat.

- Don't plant flowers in flowerbeds close to the street, as an open view across the lawn lets people see the color up close to the house. The shrubs that can be used are dwarf or slow-growing varieties that don't require constant pruning. Japanese holly (*Ilex crenata* 'Compacta'), dwarf rhododendrons, compact azaleas (*Rhododendron impeditum* and kurume azaleas), and pygmy barberry (*Berberis thunbergii* 'Crimson Pygmy') are good examples of compact, low-maintenance shrubs.

Shortcut 6: Outline the Boundaries

Strong borders are more important in the formal landscape than in the more casual styles. When a front yard is covered with a lot of cement because it has a three-car garage and super-wide driveway, an effort to break up the expanse of gray should be made by inserting brick paving stones or other texture

MISTAKES TO AVOID FOR A LOW-MAINTENANCE FORMAL/ESTATE LANDSCAPE

❖ If low maintenance is your goal, don't crowd the area with too many plants or quick-growing ground covers. The lush, overplanted jungle look takes a lot of pruning to keep it under control.

❖ Eliminating a lawn eliminates weekly mowing, but in a very formal front yard, a patch of green lawn can take the place of a lot of green plants and shrubs. If you can afford to pay for lawn care, grass is a low-maintenance option.

❖ If you have a large front yard and a formal house, consider a circular driveway as a low-maintenance, lawn-reducing option.

❖ In a formal flowerbed near the house, try to limit the different varieties in bloom. A block or mass of color is more formal than a mixture of colors and flower shapes.

❖ Don't plant deciduous trees with large leaves or messy fruits in a formal front yard, or you'll spend a lot of time raking leaves and sweeping the cement areas.

❖ Use borders, walls, and accents that relate to the material used to build the house. In the example, brick was used, but if the house is faced with stone or stucco, the garden walls, raised planter, and lamp posts next to the driveway should be constructed from the same stone or plaster finish.

treatments that can be stamped into wet cement. This is not a shortcut for the do-it-yourselfer, but is a point to consider when new construction is being planned. The driveway and courtyard in the front can be trimmed with brick insets.

- ❖ Install cement or brick curbing around the lawn to eliminate edging and to make the grass appear greener and tidier between mowings.

- ❖ Add a decorative border of brick along the cement path that leads to the front door.

Shortcut 7: Add a Whimsical Accent

In this formal/estate-style front yard, a touch of whimsy must be very subtle — no painted-plywood animals or old boots used as containers for this formal look!

- ❖ Add a cement cherub or stone bird sitting on the brick wall.

- ❖ When walls are added to a landscape, it is a great opportunity to inset decorative tiles or hanging artwork secured in cement. A cement plaque of birds could be set into the front of a brick planter. The bird theme can be continued with a stone bird sitting on the nearby wall. Tiny bird footprints could also be scratched into wet cement nearby. Using a cherub or rose motif in the plaque and as accents is another possibility.

Make-Over 3: A Drought-Resistant Contemporary/Oriental Landscape

The demand for drought-resistant landscapes is growing in tandem with water restrictions across the country. Less lawn means less water to keep it green, and many homeowners are requesting front yard designs that don't include lawns. A contemporary/Oriental style landscape easily adapts to this requirement, but the design described here also uses a front yard courtyard that borrows from the Mediterranean style of design and plant material that leans toward a desert look. Remember that the most interesting landscapes are those that combine the Oriental/contemporary style with the Mediterranean/desert look.

Shortcut 1: Get Organized

A house with a low roofline is a good candidate because it is similar to the Oriental style. Rocks and boulders can be used in place of plants. Other considerations are creating shade without resorting to thirsty shade trees and adding a dry streambed to the yard to suggest the illusion of water.

❖ Map out the location of a dry streambed and the path to the front door. Determine the location of a screening fence and overhead shade structure.

❖ Make a list of all the drought-resistant plants that can survive in your area. Visit nurseries to become acquainted with ornamental grasses and shrubs that can survive on rainfall water only.

❖ Call around to get bids on giant stepping-stones or poured concrete squares to use in place of a solid cement pathway.

❖ Gather information on sources of large boulders and the names of companies that transport boulders and position them in landscapes.

Shortcut 2: Improve the Front Entry

❖ Place large stepping-stones or blocks of textured concrete in a staggered pattern toward the front door.

❖ Add an exposed aggregate bowl near the doorway to fill with pots of blooming plants.

❖ Choose a contemporary wall hanging or highly textured wall sculpture to adorn the wall next to the door.

❖ Cover the front stoop with a large sisal or woven-grass floor mat.

Shortcut 3: Create a Vista

❖ Install a dry streambed in the front that leads the eye to the artwork on the wall near the door.

❖ Group three large boulders along the pathway to the front door. Make sure at least one-third of each boulder is buried underground for a natural look.

❖ Install a gravel spur pathway that leads toward the simple arch.

Shortcut 4: Use Nonliving Focal Points

Wall art and an exposed aggregate or stone planter can be added near the front door.

❖ Outdoor seating can be added, using an arbor overhead for shade. The bench might be made from a slab of rock laid across two concrete blocks.

❖ Construct a bridge over a dry streambed as a focal point in the center of the garden.

❖ Place gigantic boulders off to the side of the main view of the house to create a rock garden area.

Shortcut 5: Spotlight Show-Off Plants

There are two collections of plants in this garden: the tall, bushy and grassy plants grouped on one side of the dry streambed and the low-growing sedums and cacti on the other. The influence of the Japanese style and the drought-resistant nature of these plants determine the lack of mass color and green walls in this landscape style. A garden like this depends on texture and foliage color more than on flowers to achieve a show garden look.

❖ Put the bigger plants to one side of the streambed so that the groupings progress from taller to shorter. Arrange a triangle of rounded bushy plants to flow into a triangle of wispy blue fescue, which then flows into an even lower planting of trailing creeping plants. Strive for a contrast in shape and color among this trio of different plant varieties.

❖ Many of the drought-resistant plants have gray or light-colored foliage. Be sure the mulch around the plants is not the same color as the plants themselves. Use dark-colored rock or wood chips to contrast with the light-colored plants.

❖ Plant a pocket garden of low-growing succulents and thymes that will creep along the opposite side of the streambed between the staggered stepping-stones. Keep these plants in groups or colonies, emphasizing the differences in colors and textures by placing the specimens that contrast the most closest to one another. Fill in the empty spaces with rocks and gravel while you wait for the collection to spread.

❖ Add a group of boulders, small bulbs, or blooming cacti around the base of the large background tree to draw more attention to it.

❖ Plant a vine to cover the shade structure positioned over the bench in the front courtyard. Wisteria is a good drought-resistant vine in almost any climate, whereas bougainvillea thrives and blooms in mild-winter areas.

Shortcut 6: Outline the Boundaries

In a drought-resistant or contemporary/Oriental landscape, the walkways and paths make up a large part of the garden. In some landscapes, there is no front lawn, so the pathways are wider to create the flat expanse of openness that a thirsty lawn would have provided.

❖ Install a screening fence across the front courtyard. Use horizontal siding that matches the siding used on the house, or build a traditional fence but add a roof hip to give it an Oriental influence.

❖ Add thick lengths of rope or chain to the fence posts alongside the dry streambed, but leave an opening for the gravel path that leads from the bridge to the side of the house.

❖ Attach an archway to the side of the house, then install a wall that matches the screening fence in the front.

Shortcut 7: Add a Whimsical Accent

In a contemporary landscape, a piece of modern art or colorful painted tiles embedded in the garden walls or some stepping-stones can provide subtle indications of the owners' personalities.

❖ Invest in a stone fish or turtle to live in the dry streambed.

❖ Set up a fishing pole (without the hook) and arrange it for fishing from the bridge.

❖ If you have concrete poured for the giant stepping-stones, step into the damp concrete to leave footprints that lead your guests to the doorway.

❖ Play up the water theme with outdoor lighting near the pathway and streambed. Choose light fixtures that resemble the style used on docks or boats.

MISTAKES TO AVOID FOR A DROUGHT-RESISTANT, CONTEMPORARY/ORIENTAL LANDSCAPE

❖ Don't just lay gravel and rock on top of the ground and call it a dry streambed. You must dig out the earth to form a shallow ditch, lay down newspaper (10 to 15 pages thick) or another weed-blocking fabric, and layer several inches of gravel and rock on top.

❖ Don't line up rocks or boulders in neat rows sitting on top of the soil. If you want a natural look, bury at least one-third of the rock in the ground and stagger the boulders randomly throughout the landscape.

❖ Don't expect drought-resistant plants to survive the first summer without supplemental water. Newly planted trees and shrubs need time to establish a root system before they can survive a drought. Protect and tend to the needs of all new plants for at least a year after transplantation.

❖ Plant thyme and succulents around the stepping-stones, but don't be shy about pruning: It renews the growth of these low growers.

❖ Don't forget to provide shade for a seating area and front door. In sunny climates, the hot sun can ruin painted surfaces and exposed wood.

❖ Don't try to lift large boulders or transport them in a wheelbarrow. Roll them instead onto a tarp and drag them to the hole you have dug, use a stout pole as a fulcrum, and roll them into place.

Make-Over 4: A Naturalistic/Woodland Landscape to Attract Wildlife

This landscape style works best when there are large, mature trees on the property and wooded areas nearby, but even city dwellers can adapt these landscaping ideas and attract more wildlife. These homeowners enjoy the color of birds, butterflies, and other wildlife as much as they do that of flowers, so native shrubs and wildflowers are emphasized more than traditional garden flowers.

If there is no front lawn and one is necessary, shade-tolerant grasses can be substituted for the center stump and pathways.

Acquiring Native Plants

Going to the woods and digging up all that you see is not the way to collect native plant material. Not only does this destroy local ecosystems and native plants, but it also may damage the root systems beyond repair, and the plants won't survive.

Visit a local nursery and find out which native plants are commercially grown. You can then purchase a plant already growing in a pot with a tidy, compact root system. The nursery owner can tell you which commercially grown plants are related to the natives in your area. Native plants feed native animals, so attracting birds and other wildlife is as easy as providing them with plants that grow naturally in the area. This garden style should be left a little rugged and rough around the edges. Fallen branches, rotting stumps, and decaying leaves provide shelter and hiding places for the animals you want to attract.

If the wildlife in your area tends to be mainly deer, you may want to discourage them once the novelty wears off. No plant is guaranteed to be deer-proof in time of famine, but certain plants are usually left alone by wandering deer. Choose plants with thorns, such as barberry, holly, or mahonia; plants with stiff, prickly foliage, such as juniper, yew, or potentilla; or perennials that taste bitter, such as bamboo, aster, begonia, narcissus, and iris.

The plants that attract birds have berries or insects. Woodpeckers love rotting bark that is filled with larvae. Any plant that bears red berries, such as mountain ash, holly, and cotoneaster invites flocks of hungry birds.

Shortcut 1: Get Organized

A house with an A-frame roof and wood siding is a good candidate for a naturalistic landscape design. The peak in the front of the house is a natural focal point and a good shape to echo in the landscaping structures. A lot wooded with large evergreen trees casts dappled shade over the property and their extensive root systems make growing a lawn difficult.

❖ Decide which trees to keep and which to remove. Have trees that are diseased or damaged inspected by an arborist to determine whether they are in danger of falling.

❖ Sketch or walk the property, planning the natural location for paths and groups of shrubs.

Shortcut 2: Improve the Front Entry

❖ If the porch area is exposed to the elements, add a peaked porch roof that echoes the pointed roofline above.

❖ Add a wide deck with natural peeled logs to serve as a railing.

❖ Buy or build cedar or other wood planters to use for container gardens on the porch. Fill them with casual sprawling plants such as nasturtium, alyssum, lobelia, and native fern.

❖ Add window boxes with carved fronts sitting on wooden brackets, and use light-colored flowers or variegated ivy to stand out against the dark wood.

❖ Leave the wooden doors natural or stain them to match the house. You can also spruce them up with a fresh coat of wood sealer or preservative.

Shortcut 3: Create a Vista

❖ Lay a path to a pocket garden to attract birds. Use planks or boards set into the soil with moss growing in between them to lead the eye toward a bird-feeding area.

Shortcut 4: Use Nonliving Focal Points

❖ Bring in and stabilize a stump in the center of the main pathway. A stump with a pointed top echoes the pointed roofline of the house. If the only stump available is one with a flat top, drill a hole in the center, stick a pole or dowel down this hole and mount an A-frame birdhouse on top.

❖ A bird-feeding pocket garden off to the side of the porch can be made up of several nonliving focal points. Choose a trio of bird feeders to use in this area and use round log slices to make a weed-blocking base or patio below.

❖ Add rustic twig chairs for seating, pairing them with a matching twig planter.

Shortcut 5: Spotlight Show-Off Plants

This tip is hard to follow in a naturalistic garden because the plants all tend to blend in with one another, as nature intended.

❖ Plant Korean dogwood trees *(Cornus kousa)* away from the roots of evergreens but still in filtered shade.

❖ When the dogwoods are in bloom, visit the nursery for a trio of low-growing rhododendrons or azaleas that are also in flower. Add these plants to the base of the dogwoods.

❖ Plant bulbs that naturalize in drifts along the path to the front door. Note which native shrubs start to leaf out early in spring and plant crocus or snowdrop bulbs in this area to draw attention to the delicate new foliage.

❖ Add native ferns to the base of large trees and around the stump. Weed out any other plants from these areas so that the leaf patterns of the ferns can dominate against the trunks of the trees.

❖ Add a ground cover with berries (cotoneaster or kinnikinnick) to the bird garden area and plant a hedge of blueberries in this area as well.

Shortcut 6: Outline the Boundaries

A clean, dressed-up look isn't the goal of this landscape style, but strong borders help to define the different areas and change the property from a wooded lot to a native plant garden.

- ❖ Use fallen logs, peeled poles, or landscape timbers to line the main path.

- ❖ Use large rocks or wood rounds set on edge along smaller side paths.

- ❖ Install a split-rail fence around the front garden area, using post-and-board construction or laying the cedar rails across one another in a staggered pattern.

- ❖ Build a rustic archway over the main entrance to the garden.

MISTAKES TO AVOID FOR A NATURALISTIC/WOODLAND LANDSCAPE

- ❖ Don't try to make your pathways perfectly straight or the exact same width. A gentle curve or zigzag blends well with the woodland style.

- ❖ Don't use smooth cement or bricks in a tree-filled garden. Bricks grow moss and become slippery, and cement is difficult to keep free of falling needles and debris. Wood and bark chips are the most practical mulch materials for this garden style. Any cement surfaces should be of exposed aggregate or highly textured.

- ❖ Don't paint anything white. Window trim, fences, and garden accents are sure to turn green with algae and moss in a shaded woodland garden.

- ❖ Don't place the bird garden out of sight of a window, or you'll miss out on all the best viewing.

- ❖ Don't use plants that the slugs love to eat. Hostas and primroses are two shade-loving woodland plants that demand constant protection from slugs.

- ❖ Don't line the plants up in rows even if you are creating a hedge planting. Stagger the plants to make a natural-looking wall of green with more depth.

Shortcut 7: Add a Whimsical Accent

The woodland garden style offers many opportunities for whimsy. Recycled machinery parts and weathered containers look right at home.

❖ Display a collection of birdhouses on the arch, on the stump, and in the bird garden.

❖ Use a decorative feature as a place to hang apples and suet for the birds.

❖ Carve the steps up to the front porch from giant logs laid on their sides and coated with a glossy wood preservative. Go ahead and carve your initials.

❖ Display wood carvings outdoors nailed to fence posts and stumps.

Show Gardens: The Best Locations for Inspiration

Some of us are lucky enough to live in an area blooming with beautiful show gardens, either as part of a public park system or historical museum. There are also private show gardens that are open to the public on certain days. The list of gardens below includes only the largest and most well-known showcase gardens in this country and parts of Canada.

Any garden lover lucky enough to visit Europe or the Far East should investigate the famous gardens in these other parts of the world as well. Remember that ideas for plant and color combinations, building material, and garden layout can be adapted from any place people group together plants to form a garden. Your own city or neighborhood should be the place to start collecting ideas immediately. Local garden spots are also the most practical place to learn about the plant material that will survive in your climate.

Before you fill up the gas tank and head for one of these distant horticultural wonders, make sure you phone ahead to check the hours, admission price, and driving directions. You could also inquire about the size of the garden, areas of specialty, and how much time to allow yourself to tour the grounds. These kinds of questions may help you decide if an out-of-the way show garden is worth the trip.

If you'd like to really make the most of your visit, be prepared, and take a notebook and camera. In most cases, you'll be dazzled with so many great ideas that they'll all blur together once you get back home. A few notes or even some postcards from the gift shop will help refresh your memory. Don't worry yet about finding a good location on your own property for the perennial pairings or Victorian porch swing you admired at a show garden. Just make a note in your idea book that daylillies and feverfew are a comfortable couple or that a porch swing hung on the side of a garage dresses up a blank wall. You may not have that blank wall or a sunny spot for perennials now, but when a house addition or the removal of some trees begs for relandscaping, you'll be armed with a source of good ideas. The point is to absorb and take note of what you like. Record not only what catches your eye, but what is planted around the same type of tree that you have in your yard, or the way a slope is landscaped. The more gardens you visit, the more developed your own personal taste will become. You'll be discovering what landscape style appeals to you the most.

Visiting beautiful gardens shouldn't be all study and note-taking. Remember that pleasure and beauty are the reason that ornamental gardens are planted in the first place. Take every opportunity as you go through life to appreciate beauty, in whatever form it appears.

ALABAMA

Bellingrath Gardens
Theodore, AL
(205) 973–2217
Over 65 acres of formal gardens with lots of color throughout the year. There are almost a thousand more acres of native trees and shrubs.

ALASKA

Museum of Alaska Transportation and Industry
Palmer, AK
(902) 745–4493
A garden of flowerbeds that surrounds a museum in the small town of Palmer, the blooming plants will help any new gardener in the area learn about what plants will flower in this state with harsh winters and short summers.

ARIZONA

Desert Botanical Garden
Phoenix, AZ
(602) 941–1225
A series of pathways leads visitors through 150 acres of native plants and landscape plants. Demonstration areas teach homeowners about water conservation and the people and animals of the Sonoran Desert.

Sharlot Hall Museum
Prescott, AZ
(602) 445–3122.
A Victorian-style governor's mansion is adorned with an herb garden, a rose garden, and vegetable beds containing heirloom plants. These gardens provide a good example of how a traditional home can be landscaped even in arid conditions.

CALIFORNIA

Los Angeles State and County Arboretum
Arcadia, CA
(818) 446–8251
This extensive collection of plant materials is grown on 127 acres just 15 miles from Los Angeles. A large herb garden, rose garden, and some of the best examples of waterfalls and pond gardens are represented.

Huntington Botanical Gardens
San Marino, CA
(818) 449–3901
These impressive show gardens are built around an art gallery and include a rose garden, Italian-style lawn area, herb garden, and a 5-acre Japanese garden including a Zen garden of sand and rock. The entire complex fills 200 acres with collections of palms, camellias, and an unusual Australian garden.

Golden Gate Park
San Francisco, CA
(415) 661–1316
More than 1,000 acres allow visitors to gather ideas from the fuchsia garden, camellia garden, Japanese garden, and many other styles. The mild climate of this area means a wide variety of plant material can be showcased.

Balboa Park
San Diego, CA
(619) 239–0512
Formal garden areas including a Moorish-style and a Spanish garden are beautifully maintained alongside the English garden, Rose garden, Desert garden, and others. This park and its gardens have been inspiring home landscapers for more than 100 years.

Filoli
Woodside, CA
(415) 364–3880
This is the image most gardeners conjure up when they picture a show garden. Originally built as the showcase gardens to surround the mansion of a millionaire, Filoli is designed in the formal, elegant European style. There are four major garden "rooms," including a sunken garden, walled garden, woodland garden, and panel garden. Unlike most parks and arboretums, Filoli has landscaping examples that are easy to adapt to the home landscape — if you like the formal estate look. Advance reservations are required!

Sunset Magazine Gardens
Menlo Park, CA
(415) 321–3600
If you're familiar with Sunset magazine and the landscape ideas they present for Western gardeners, then you'll understand why a visit to the magazine test gardens is inspiring. Year-round color is achieved with display beds, but the real reason to visit these gardens is to note the practical, labor-, and water-saving techniques that the magazine is famous for teaching.

Hearst San Simeon State Historical Monument
San Simeon, CA
(800) 444-4445
The famous Hearst Castle was once the home of newspaper publisher, William Randolph Hearst. Perched high above the Pacific, tours through the mansion itself take 4 hours, and the gardens have only recently been opened to the public. The transporting of soil, trees, and fine works of art to the sight is a horticultural feat that make the humble homeowner grateful for simple problems such as poor drainage. This estate is another fine example of the formal garden style, but much of it is so grand and awesome that the ideas are hard to adapt to your own back yard. Take the time to visit it anyway, just to see one of the most impressive residences in the world. San Simeon is located about halfway between San Francisco and Los Angelos along the coastal highway.

COLORADO
Denver Botanic Gardens
Denver, CO
(303) 575-2547
If your property has a lot of rocks, a tour of the 4-acre rock alpine garden will be a highlight of your visit to the 22-acre Denver Botanic garden. There are 14 other theme gardens in the complex including herbs, roses, perennials, a Japanese garden, and good examples of xeriscaping or landscaping with water conservation in mind.

Mineral Palace Park
Pueblo, CO
(719) 543-4005
If it's color you're after, a tour of this park will leave you satisfied if you visit during the spring or summer season. Flowering annuals and roses, along with a collection of subtropical and tropical plants in a pair of greenhouses makes this 50-acre park worth a visit.

DELAWARE
Nemours Foundation
Wilmington, DE
(303) 573-3333
This 300-acre estate was designed with show gardens to complement the Louis XIV style mansion. The gardens are very formal and impressive.

Winterthur Gardens
Wilmington, DE
(302) 654-1548
Another huge estate that is beautifully landscaped and now open to the public. Winterthur has a formal garden area, but also showcases a more natural look with an azalea garden, lawn areas, and blooming shrubs that any homeowner could use. There is a gift shop and mail-order catalog that make falling in love with something at Winterthur easy because you can order some of the choice plants and outdoor art work by mail. (See Appendix B.)

DISTRICT OF COLUMBIA
Dumbarton Oaks and Gardens
Washington, DC
(202) 342–3290
The landscaping of this estate will inspire home gardeners to use more brick, stone and pebbles. There is also much to be learned by the excellent use of plants that add spring and autumn color.

HAWAII
Waimea Falls Park Arboretum
Oahu, Haleiwa, HI
(808) 638–8655
The tropical beauty of Hawaii is represented in more than 30 specialty gardens spread across this beautiful valley. Even if you garden far from the tropics and could never grow the tender plants represented, visiting the many gardens in Hawaii will teach garden lovers about the use of water and layering of lush plant material.

There are many other show gardens in this state, but the tourist industry does such a good job of providing information that traveling gardeners are encouraged to contact a travel agent for more information on the horticulture displays of this area.

LOUISIANA
Live Oak Gardens and Joseph Jefferson Home
New Iberia, LA
(318) 367–3485
This is a show garden built around the mansion of Joseph Jefferson and showing the elegance and splendor of the old south.

A Japanese garden, roses, perennials, and thousands of spring bulbs add lots of color to the lovely grounds.

MISSOURI
Missouri Botanical Garden
St. Louis, MO
(314) 577–5100
The arboretum and botanical gardens encompass nearly 3,000 acres and include the largest indoor planting in this country beneath the cover of a geodesic dome. The many plant collections teach the home landscaper about grouping together similar plants.

NEW YORK
New York Botanical Garden
Bronx, NY
(212) 220–8728
Aside from an extensive collection of plant material, this famous garden also contains a rock garden, rose garden, large herb garden, and a conservatory.

Brooklyn Botanic Garden
Brooklyn, NY
(212) 622–4433
In this city location you can study three Japanese gardens, a fragrance garden, Iris and Magnolia gardens, and a Bonsai collection. There's also a conservatory filled with color.

Old Westbury Gardens
Old Westbury, NY
(516) 333–0048
A Georgian mansion on Long Island has been opened to the public, and the spectacular landscaping on this property is internationally admired. There are five separate garden areas and long avenues of trees framing the water.

NORTH CAROLINA
Biltmore Estate and Gardens
Asheville, NC
(704) 274–1776
The mountain top site is spectacular enough, but the formal French-style château and expansive gardens make this one of the most showy of all show gardens. An Italian garden, walled garden, and large shrub garden inspire even the beginning gardener.

OREGON
Japanese Garden
Portland, OR
(503) 223–4070
This is the one of the best examples of the Japanese-style of landscaping outside of Japan. The 5½ acres are broken down into several garden areas, including a strolling pond garden, a tea garden, and low-maintenance, drought-tolerant but serene and beautiful sand and stone garden. It's a real treasure not to be missed.

Portland International Rose Test Garden
Portland, OR
(503) 248–4302
Portland is known as the city of roses, and this public garden shows why. There are plenty of other plantings besides roses including tulips, azaleas, and a Shakespearean garden with trees, brick walks, and a lot of summer-blooming plants. It's an excellent place to decide which are your favorite roses before starting a rose garden of your own.

PENNSYLVANIA
Longwood Gardens
Kennett Square, PA
(215) 388–6741
Established by Pierre S. DuPont, these outstanding gardens cover more than 1,000 acres and include water gardens, fountains, conservatories, and a spectacular arboretum. Longwood Gardens is considered to be the best show garden in the country.

Swiss Pines Park
Malvern, PA
(215) 933–6916
Gardeners that want to use native or naturalized plant groupings can glean ideas from this park, as well as Japanese garden plans, rhododendron plantings, herbs, and rose gardens. This park also contains an unusual Polynesian garden.

RHODE ISLAND

The Breakers
Newport, RI
(401) 847–1000
Another example of a mansion with estate gardens, this one was built for Cornelius Vanderbilt and overlooks the Atlantic Ocean. The gardens are formal but very well designed.

The Elms
Newport, RI
(401) 847–1000
The mansion and gardens are extravagant and done in the formal French style. The sunken gardens should inspire homeowners to take a shovel to the back-yard and put in one of their own.

SOUTH CAROLINA

Festival of Houses and Gardens
Charleston, SC
(803) 723–1623
The Historic Charleston Foundation sponsors spring walking tours of downtown Charleston, and visiting actual homes and well-cared-for gardens is probably the best way to gather usable ideas for landscape improvement. For more information you can also write to the Foundation's headquarters at 51 Meeting Street, Charleston, SC 29401.

TENNESSEE

The Hermitage
Nashville, TN
(615) 889–2941
The former home of President Andrew Jackson, this working plantation has been beautifully restored and the fine gardens are definitely worth emulating.

UTAH

Temple Gardens
Salt Lake City, UT
(801) 531–2640
The meticulously maintained gardens around the Mormon temple are full of usable ideas for color and theme garden areas. The designs show a refreshing originality.

VIRGINIA

Monticello
Charlottesville, VA
(804) 295–8181
The well-known gardens designed by Thomas Jefferson have been restored as closely as possible to Jefferson's original plan. The wide expanse of lawn edged with trees and shrubs is a style suburban homeowners can easily imitate. Even the flower borders feature hardy annuals and perennials that demand less care than the more formal bedfellows found in other show gardens.

Colonial Williamsburg
Williamsburg, VA
(804) 229–1000
A recreation of small-town life in the colonies is beautifully planted in the village scene of colonial Williamsburg. The small kitchen gardens and herb beds are easy to adapt to city lots.

WASHINGTON

Rhododendron Species Foundation Garden
Federal Way, WA
(206) 927–6960
The largest collection of species rhododendrons in the country make this woodland path garden a good example of how to work with rhododendrons, azaleas, and other shade-tolerant plants. The gardens are on land donated by the nearby Weyerhauser corporation and also includes an impressive bonsai collection. Homeowners who have tall trees and filtered shade on the property should visit these gardens to fully appreciate the potential that shade offers.

University of Washington Arboretum
Seattle, WA
(206) 625–2635
This 250-acre arboretum makes great use of azaleas and flowering cherry trees, but the true star is the 3-acre Japanese garden situated around a pond.

Point Defiance Park
Tacoma, WA
(206) 759–0118
This outstanding park fills more than 600 acres with native plants, an aquarium, and a zoo, but also inspires home landscapers with its Japanese garden, rose garden, and colorful beds.

CANADA

Minter Gardens
P.O. Box 40
Chilliwacka, BC
(604) 794–7191
Set amidst the natural beauty of British Columbia, Minter gardens is a well-planned and beautifully maintained show garden with a woodlands area, children's garden, perennial gardens, rose garden, aviary, and many other theme garden areas. It is located close to the Washington-Canadian border.

The Butchart Gardens
P.O. Box 4010
Victoria, BC
(604) 652–5256
A spectacular display of mature plants and colorful annuals attract thousands of tourists to the sunken gardens, herb gardens, rose gardens, Japanese garden, and old quarry garden (that was once an eyesore and reclaimed and replanted to become the focal point of these prestigious show gardens). Every garden lover must make a pilgrimage to The Butchart Gardens at least once.

APPENDIX B

Sources of Supply

When I die and go to heaven, I imagine my arrival to be like stepping into the pages of one of these garden catalogs. The gardens in paradise will surely be decked out with shiny tools that never rust, birdbaths that are never scummy, and choice plants that are always in lush, beautiful bloom. Your local nursery or garden center is likely to carry a variety of plants and equipment.

The mail-order companies listed below can send you color catalogs from which to order benches, arches, plants, weathervanes, sundials, or any other type of garden focal point imaginable. Even if you're too practical to consider a carved wood bench or cast iron Victorian-style pot, you can still use these catalogs as a form of cheap entertainment. All but one of them can be mailed to you free for the asking. This is only a partial listing. *The Complete Guide to Gardening by Mail* is available from The Mailorder Association of Nurseries, Dept. SCI, 8683 Doves Fly Way, Laurel, MD 20723. Please add $1.00 for postage and handling in the United States ($1.50 for Canada).

Expensive embellishments are not the only specialty of these mail-order garden suppliers. Down-to-earth gardening aids such as shovels, gloves, watering systems, and fertilizers are also offered, and some of them are priced lower than what you would pay at the local hardware store. Labor-saving gadgets are also well represented, so you can garden with less perspiration and more inspiration just by flipping your green thumbs through these pages.

Alsto's Handy Helpers
P.O. Box 1267
Galesburg, IL 61401
(800) 447-0048
Alsto's offers classic garden furniture and ornaments, accessories, container plants, and gift items.

Gardener's Eden
Box 7303
San Francisco, CA 94120-7307
(800) 822-9600
Offers many gift items appropriate for gardeners and some nice ornamental shrubs and outdoor containers. This company is owned by Williams-Sonoma.

Gardener's Supply Company
128 Intervale Road
Burlington, VT 05401
(800) 955-3370
Innovative gardening products including accessories, ornaments, equipment, and gift items.

Jackson and Perkins
P.O. Box 1028
Medford, OR 97501
(800) 292–4769
Well known for roses, Jackson and Perkins also sells perennials, trees, and shrubs as well as an impressive collection of traditional garden ornaments. This is the best place to order mini-tree roses.

Kinsman Company
River Road
Point Pleasant, PA 18950
(800) 733-5613
Kinsman Company has fine-quality tools and equipment but is also known for its wonderful black steel modular arches. They are easy to set up in the garden, are less expensive, and require less maintenance than anything you'll find locally.

The Plow and Hearth
301 Madison Road
Orange, VA 22960
(800) 866-6072
This catalog also offers fireplace tools, outdoor furniture, and pet supplies, as well as beautiful accessories for the garden.

Smith and Hawken
25 Corte Madera
Mill Valley, CA 94941
(800) 776-3336
Smith and Hawken offers not only great tools to lean casually against your shed for display purposes, but gardening pants, shirts, hats, and carrying baskets as well as the perfect bench or outdoor ornament.

Stonecrafters
901 33rd Street North
Birmingham, AL 35222
(800) 325-1253
This is the one company on the list whose wholesale catalog of stone garden ornaments costs $5.00. As the name implies, these folks make heavy-duty cast-stone garden ornaments, planters, birdbaths, ornaments and statuary to grace the most impressive show gardens.

White Flower Farm
Litchfield, CT 06759-0050
(203) 496–9624
Although this established mail-order company is best known for its beautiful color catalog of perennials, they have also introduced a holiday catalog, Gifts for Gardeners and Their Friends. Although many of the gifts would better decorate your indoors than outdoors, there are some charming windchimes and herbal topiary plants offered that might be just the accent your garden needs.

Winterthur Museum
Gardens Catalogue Division
115 Brand Road
Salem, VA 24156
(800) 848–2929
Winterthur is a real historic show garden and museum that sells reproductions and adaptions of the birdbaths, sundials, and statuary that adorns the grounds. Also offers choice shrubs, some of them taken from cuttings of plants growing at Wintherthur.

Index